Decolonizing Literature

Decolonizing the Curriculum

Anna Bernard, *Decolonizing Literature*
Ali Meghji, *Decolonizing Sociology*
Robbie Shilliam, *Decolonizing Politics*
Sarah A. Radcliffe, *Decolonizing Geography*

Decolonizing Literature

An Introduction

Anna Bernard

polity

Copyright © Anna Bernard 2023

The right of Anna Bernard to be identified as Author of this Work has been asserted in accordance with the UK Copyright, Designs and Patents Act 1988.

First published in 2023 by Polity Press

Polity Press
65 Bridge Street
Cambridge CB2 1UR, UK

Polity Press
111 River Street
Hoboken, NJ 07030, USA

All rights reserved. Except for the quotation of short passages for the purpose of criticism and review, no part of this publication may be reproduced, stored in a retrieval system or transmitted, in any form or by any means, electronic, mechanical, photocopying, recording or otherwise, without the prior permission of the publisher.

ISBN-13: 978-1-5095-4462-2
ISBN-13: 978-1-5095-4463-9 (pb)

A catalogue record for this book is available from the British Library.

Library of Congress Control Number: 2022951512

Typeset in 10.5 on 12.5pt Sabon
by Fakenham Prepress Solutions, Fakenham, Norfolk NR21 8NL
Printed and bound in the UK by CPI Group (UK) Ltd, Croydon

The publisher has used its best endeavours to ensure that the URLs for external websites referred to in this book are correct and active at the time of going to press. However, the publisher has no responsibility for the websites and can make no guarantee that a site will remain live or that the content is or will remain appropriate.

Every effort has been made to trace all copyright holders, but if any have been overlooked the publisher will be pleased to include any necessary credits in any subsequent reprint or edition.

For further information on Polity, visit our website:
politybooks.com

Contents

Acknowledgements	vi
Introduction	1
1 Decolonization and Literature: A History	11
2 Unfinished Business: How Do We Decolonize Literature?	33
3 Language and Translation: What Is 'English' Literature?	54
4 'A Comparative Literature of Imperialism': Reading Colonial and Anticolonial Texts Together	78
5 Telling a Collective Story: Literature and Anticolonial Struggle	102
6 Decolonizing Genre: Anticolonial Understandings of Literary Craft	127
Conclusion	151
Notes	156
References	160
Index	180

Acknowledgements

I wrote this book during the global disaster of the COVID-19 pandemic and the personal adventure of the early years of my daughter's life. It would never have been finished without the support of my brilliant and generous colleagues, students, friends, and family. Much of it began life in the classroom, and I'm especially grateful to my students in the Departments of Comparative Literature and English at King's College London and the Department of English and Related Literature at the University of York, as well as to colleagues I've taught alongside, including Derek Attridge, David Attwell, Jane Elliott, Ziad Elmarsafy, Anup Grewal, Michelle Kelly, Tom Langley, Caroline Laurent, Justine McConnell, Javed Majeed, Sara Marzagora, Sebastian Matzner, Emilie Morin, Zoe Norridge, Ruvani Ranasinha, and Claire Westall. The members of the King's Decolonising Working Group have been an enormous inspiration, especially Malak Abdelkhalek, Sudi Ali, Lily Beckett, Nicole Bilan, Nicholas Chua Bingkai, Kal Harris, Yawen Li, Sara Marzagora, Ishat Mirza, John Narayan, Lucia Pradella, AbdoolKarim Vakil, and Rebecca Walker. Special thanks also to my past and present doctoral students Haya Alfarhan, Dalal Alomair, Hannah Boast, Leila Essa, Isabelle Hesse, Faten Hussein, Lya Morales Hernández, Sinéad Murphy, Shadya Radhi, Nicola Robinson, Haifa Al-Rumaih, Michal Shalev, and Sutida Wimuttikosol, who are all doing their own superb work of decolonizing literature and other kinds of institutions.

Acknowledgements vii

Sincere thanks to Anthony Alessandrini, Amy De'Ath, Charles Forsdick, Madhu Krishnan, Omid Tofighian, and Jonathan Ward for sharing their work and ideas with me for this book. My thinking about how the work of decolonizing literary studies relates to collective struggles past and present has been invigorated by the commitment and insight of the members of the International Solidarity Action Research Network (isarn.org), especially Anthony Alessandrini and Jessica Stites Mor, and the Internationalism, Cosmopolitanism and the Politics of Solidarity research group at the London School of Economics, especially Ayça Çubukçu and Vidya Kumar. The scholarship of Timothy Brennan, Joe Cleary, Sharae Deckard, Ben Etherington, Priyamvada Gopal, Karima Laachir, Neil Lazarus, Caroline Rooney, Lyndsey Stonebridge, Jarad Zimbler, and the much-missed Barbara Harlow and Benita Parry has shaped how I think about the political work of literature.

I'm grateful to the Parents' and Carers' Fund at King's College London for giving me the space I needed to start work on this book when I returned from parental leave, and to Marie Berry, Stephanie Mannion, Dot Pearce, and Paul Readman for making it possible for me to do the rest of my job and still keep my spirits up. At Polity, Ellen MacDonald-Kramer, Ian Malcolm, and Pascal Porcheron provided excellent editorial guidance and support, and the anonymous reviewers helped make this a better book. Last but most of all, thanks to my wonderful family: Jim Bernard, Susan Lacy, Sara Bernard, and especially Mervyn, Gina, and Sam Love, who are everything.

Introduction

> Decolonization must offer a language of possibility, a way out of colonialism.
> Linda Tuhiwai Smith (2012 [1999])

> Decolonising the curriculum is a hot topic now, so for now, we have the moment. The moment is ours if we hold our nerve, but if we falter, the moment is lost, as are we.
> Foluke Adebisi (2019)

In April 2015, after a month of demonstrations, the University of Cape Town gave in to its students' demands and removed a statue of the British colonial administrator Cecil Rhodes from the campus. The visibility and success of this campaign – which also took place online, using the hashtag #RhodesMustFall – inspired student activists across South Africa and beyond, including at the University of Oxford, where students began a similarly high-profile campaign to remove another Rhodes statue from Oriel College. As Achille Mbembe observed at the time, the UCT activists focused on the Rhodes statue as an emblem of the racist violence and destructiveness of British colonial rule:

> Cecil Rhodes belonged to the race of men who were convinced that to be black is a liability. During his time and life in Southern Africa, he used his considerable power – political and financial – to make black people

all over Southern Africa pay a bloody price for his beliefs. ... [B]ringing Rhodes' statue down is one of the many legitimate ways in which we can, today in South Africa, demythologize that history and put it to rest. (2015, pp. 2–3)

Mbembe, like the student activists and the contemporary Black Lives Matter movement, is making the point that statues, street names, and commemorative plaques are not innocuous traces of a long-vanished empire. They represent a system of institutionalized white supremacy that took hold during centuries of European colonial rule in Africa, Asia, and the Americas and that continues to structure our economic, social, political, and cultural lives. These movements are united in their belief that the removal of such symbols is only the first step in a much longer and more difficult process of decolonization, which demands that the formal and informal structures that maintain the dominance of the former colonial powers and the prestige of whiteness are abolished, wherever they are found.

The recent student movements have also called for the decolonization of the curriculum, which is a key form in which colonial structures of thought are perpetuated in universities. While this means different things in different disciplines, there is a broad consensus among the students and teachers who are involved in this effort that, in order to begin to decolonize our curricula, we must identify and undo the colonial ideas and assumptions that underpin our fields. This means uncovering the colonial history of our disciplines and confronting the Eurocentrism of our method-ologies, objects of study, citation practices, programme structures, and syllabi. Literature students have been some of the most vocal participants in these campaigns. These students' demands are not limited to the inclusion of more Black, Brown, Indigenous, women, LGBTQ+, disabled, and working-class authors on their reading lists; they also seek fundamental changes to how literature students are taught to read and what they are encouraged to value. As Cambridge English students put it in an open letter to their faculty, this

Introduction 3

'means challenging the pervasive notion that reading texts in the light of gender, race, ability, class and so on is to crush them under the weight of subjectivity, dismantling the idea that white and male is the norm, unmarked by identity' (Fly Cambridge, 2017).

Decolonizing Literature takes its cue from such interventions, arguing that the decolonization of literary studies requires a change to not only what, but how, we read. Along with the decentring of historically dominant perspectives, this might mean a renewed attention to authors' efforts to document socio-economic conditions or persuade the reader of a particular point of view; a broader definition of literary experimentation, beyond its tacit identification with Western modernism and postmodernism; more developed strategies for reading texts in translation or in postcolonial and regional versions of European imperial languages; and more in-depth analysis of works that explicitly align themselves with anticolonial political movements or seek to imagine genuinely postcolonial futures. This book offers literature students and educators some suggestions for beginning to read in these ways, and thus to unlearn the still prevalent belief that a text's aesthetic properties can be considered separately from its politics (Jameson, 1986; Bernard, 2013, pp. 22–8).

Literature is already a high-profile site of debate about disciplinary decolonization, and some important gains have been made in the last few decades. This is due mainly to the influence of postcolonial studies, which gained an institutional footing in English literature departments in the 1980s and 1990s, as I discuss in chapter 1. Scholars aligned with this field set out to expose the imperial foundations of the idea of 'English literature' and to demonstrate its historical role in legitimizing the British empire. They also sought to remake the English literary canon by turning to texts written in English by authors from former British colonies and from metropolitan ethnic minority backgrounds. (By 'metropolitan', I mean countries that were imperial centres and still command disproportionate wealth and power, such as Britain and France, or the United States, whose ongoing global dominance means it is better described as a neo-imperial

4 Introduction

centre.) Over time, this challenge to the traditional canon has expanded to include literature in translation from other languages and from the rest of the formerly colonized world, including the Middle East/North Africa and Latin America, leading to postcolonial literature's reformulation as 'world literature' and increasingly blurring the lines between English departments and departments of comparative literature and modern languages. Meanwhile, similar attempts to interrogate the origins of the discipline and tackle its Eurocentrism have taken place in European literature studies, particularly in French departments, and in Black, Asian (especially Asian-American), Latinx, and Indigenous studies.

These efforts to diversify and decentre the canon have been moderately successful. As Neil Lazarus argued two decades ago, '[t]oday courses in post-1945 "English" literature that ignore "minority" or "postcolonial" writers and the issues of decolonization, migration, and diaspora are simply anachronistic' (2004, p. 14). In metropolitan anglophone universities, there are now very few literature departments that do not include at least one specialist in postcolonial or world literature, and most literature students will encounter some work by non-European or metropolitan ethnic minority writers and be encouraged to read canonical texts in relation to the history of empire. In some institutions, particularly in the United States, this transformation has gone even further, so that, in the post-1945 curriculum, modules that focus on texts by writers of colour, women, and/or queer writers are now in the majority. (For more discussion of current trends in university English literature teaching, see chapter 2.) But this does not mean that literary studies has been decolonized. Conventional historical periodization and 'great authors' courses continue to underpin the curriculum in many departments, even those with more diverse post-1945 coverage. Domestic ethnic minority writing is also far better represented in most English departments than writing from the rest of the world, which tends to be reserved for the fewer, smaller, and less well-resourced comparative literature and modern languages departments. Moreover, despite increased attention to the relationship between literature

Introduction 5

and political movements, modules that use words such as 'justice', 'protest', 'solidarity', or 'decolonization' in their titles or descriptions remain rare in comparison to modules organized according to group identity (African-American writing, Australian Indigenous writing, etc.). The limitations of such reforms have led scholars such as Claire Westall (2015, p. 18) to argue that postcolonial criticism allowed the wider discipline of literary studies to rehabilitate itself as a post-imperial and multicultural discipline simply by incorporating a restricted amount of 'new' material, without having to significantly change the makeup of the 'core' canon or the assumptions brought to bear on literary texts (see also Etherington and Zimbler, 2021, p. 228).

As Kavita Bhanot reminds us, such 'quick-fixes to the "diversity" problem ... ensur[e] that literature remains in the same circles of power, within one class and caste ... [W]hite literature is held up as the "real" literature that we all need to aspire towards' (2015). Bhanot is referring to the treatment of British Black and Asian writers in the British publishing industry, but her critique also applies to university literature education and research. Like the removal of the Rhodes statues, diversification of our reading lists is the start of decolonizing our discipline, not its end point. Indeed, to describe this work as decoloniz*ing* is to name decolonization as an unfinished project: it is 'not a destination' but 'a way of being' (Adebisi, 2019). We may not yet be able to envision a decolonized world, but we can develop ways of reading and thinking that help us imagine a 'way out of colonialism', as Linda Tuhiwai Smith puts it in the first epigraph to this chapter. Literature students and scholars are well placed for this task, since literary texts play a crucial role in imaginatively connecting geographically and historically distant struggles and in witnessing, instigating, and envisioning historical change (Forsdick, 2018, pp. 701–3). As readers and critics, we must take these properties of our object of study seriously and bring them to bear on what we decide to read as well as how we interpret it.

In keeping with an understanding of decolonization as an 'unfulfilled promise' and a 'utopian aspiration' (Wenzel,

6 Introduction

2017), this book defines decolonization as both a historical phenomenon and a political practice.[1] Although I discuss texts that have emerged from a range of twentieth- and twenty-first-century contexts, my key point of reference is the great wave of mid-twentieth-century struggles in Asia and Africa for independence from European rule. The national liberation movements of this period saw themselves as engaged in a common political project, as their efforts to develop a 'Third World' alternative to Euro–US imperialism and the Soviet Union show (Lee, 2010, p. 15). Today, that historical moment of decolonization seems distant: the imperial restoration of the 1970s and 1980s, facilitated by US military interventions against resistant postcolonial states, has made it hard to imagine the outcome of anticolonial revolution as anything but tragic (Lazarus, 2013, pp. 327–8; Scott, 2004). However, the idea of decolonization retains its urgency as a political outlook that takes inspiration from these struggles and seeks to continue the work they started. Ongoing practices of military invasion, economic exploitation, environmental destruction, land seizure, and political marginalization of one group or state by another are just some of the ways in which the 'unbroken history' of capitalist imperialism continues in the present. Crucially, however, the 'counter-history of resistance' to these violent appropriations continues alongside it (Lazarus, 2013, p. 337).

This understanding of decolonization as carrying on from the work of previous anticolonial resistance movements is distinct from the influential notion of the 'decolonial' as a challenge to the epistemology of Western colonial modernity. The concept of decoloniality comes from Latin American studies, particularly the work of the Argentinian theorist Walter Mignolo (2011; Mignolo and Walsh, 2018), who draws on the idea of the 'coloniality of power' proposed by the Peruvian sociologist Aníbal Quijano (2000). This approach emphasizes the inseparability of capitalist modernity from colonialism and Eurocentrism. In response, decolonial scholarship seeks to challenge the ongoing privileging of European knowledge and recover non-European intellectual and cultural histories and experience, moving beyond the

Introduction 7

anticolonial movements' perceived emphasis on political independence as the end point of decolonization. The ideas and aims of decolonial scholarship are in keeping with much of my argument in this book. However, I do not see 'decoloniality' and 'decolonization' as synonymous. As Priyamvada Gopal and Stefan Helgesson both argue, Mignolo's concept of decoloniality problematically posits a radical difference between European and non-European 'categories of thought', ahistorically construing these formations as static and discrete instead of evolving and entangled (Gopal, 2019, pp. 79–85; Helgesson, 2022, pp. 166–70). It also overlooks anticolonial liberation thinkers' own emphases on the unfulfilled revolutionary promises of liberalism and socialism (Gopal, 2019, p. 83) and their 'complex dialogue' with '"Western" thinking' (Helgesson, 2022, p. 4). Far from repudiating ideas of universality or human commonality as intrinsically 'European', members of many anticolonial movements fought to expand and reimagine these concepts (Gopal, 2019, pp. 83–4; see also Rivera Cusicanqui, 2020; Getachew and Mantena, 2021, p. 371). Like Gopal, instead of 'decolonial' I prefer the term 'anticolonial', which for me indicates the aspiration towards a common anti-imperial liberationist project carried out across many different sites of resistance, including the metropolitan centres.[2] The oppositional emphasis of the term '*anti*colonial' also foregrounds the need to take sides in an ongoing struggle.

For those who benefit from the current system by occupying a position of racial, national, class, gender, and/or other form of privilege within it, it is essential to unlearn this privilege to take part in the work of decolonization. (The need to unlearn pertains in a different way to those without such privilege whose education has nevertheless promoted an internalized white supremacy, as Ngũgĩ wa Thiong'o argues in his celebrated book *Decolonising the Mind*, discussed in chapters 1 and 3.) *Decolonizing Literature* takes the position that this unlearning – figured, like decolonizing, as an ongoing project – requires us to consider how we know what we know, how we learned it, and how we might challenge or undo it. It also requires that we read the work

8 Introduction

of writers and thinkers who have opposed capitalist imperialism and sought to represent the worldviews and lived realities of its victims and adversaries. As Ariella Azoulay puts it, 'Unlearning with companions means no longer privileging the accounts of imperial agents, scholars included, and instead retrieving other modalities of sharing the world' (2019, p. 16). *Decolonizing Literature* suggests ways that literature students and scholars might embark on this project of unlearning by laying out some of the work that has already been done and asking readers to think about where we go from here.

Chapter 1 summarizes colonialism's impact on the discipline and outlines the work of key figures in postcolonial literary studies. Alongside this institutional history, the chapter also introduces landmark interventions in the decolonization of literary studies by explicitly anticolonial writers and scholars. Chapter 2 encourages readers to reflect on their own experiences of literary study and to think about how they might continue the work of decolonizing the university literature curriculum. Chapters 3 to 6 introduce four key ways of decolonizing literary studies – attention to language, comparative and contrapuntal reading, reading for political argument, and attention to genre – accompanied by discussions of literary and critical texts that illustrate and support each idea. The conclusion reiterates the need to transform both what and how we read, connecting this demand to current global crises and to the reader's own responsibilities as a reader and critic.

The selection of texts and themes is most directly relevant to the decolonization of English literature departments in the metropolitan anglophone academy, reflecting my own academic formation and my institutional location in English and Comparative Literature departments in a British university. However, the alternative principles for choosing and interpreting texts that I suggest challenge more widely held assumptions about the work of literature and literary critics, which is why the book's title refers to 'literature' rather than 'English literature'. The coverage is far from comprehensive: Caribbean, African, and Arab writers are better

Introduction 9

represented than writers from the rest of the world, and I pay more attention to issues of race, nation, and political belief than class, gender, sexuality, or disability. I also engage much more with texts in English and English translation than in other languages, though where possible I have consulted the original versions of texts first published in Spanish, French, or Arabic. I hope that the book will encourage readers with interests in other literatures, languages, and topics to think about approaches that might be most relevant for their areas of focus.

As I wrote this book, the risk of co-opting the struggle to decolonize was always on my mind. The idea of decolonization has acquired considerable market value in recent years, as the profusion of academic books with 'decolonizing' in the title (including this one) suggests. As Madhu Krishnan (2019) has observed, the cachet that is now associated with this term has allowed it to be appropriated by those who seek to maintain their own institutional standing while silencing the voices of those who have been on the front lines of decolonizing work, who are often Black or Brown, women, and/or precariously employed academics and students. As a white academic with an open-ended university position, I am keenly aware that I benefit from the structures that this book seeks to dislodge. I have sought throughout to foreground the work of writers and thinkers who have led the way in political and cultural decolonization struggles, many of them from Black, Indigenous, Arab, Latinx, and Asian metropolitan and non-metropolitan backgrounds. The book thus seeks to respond to Foluke Adebisi's invitation, in the second epigraph to this chapter, to use decolonization's current status as a 'hot topic' to help make the changes that we want to see in our institutions and our disciplines. In order to decolonize literary studies, I contend, we must take the political work of literature seriously. We must grapple with texts that overtly challenge imperialism and capitalism and reject the artificial separation of aesthetics from politics in our interpretations of all texts. We must also remember that decolonization is not a top-down initiative but a collaborative process. This work begins by putting our own locations and sources of knowledge into dialogue with others and by ensuring that everything is up for debate, especially the question of what makes a 'good' work of literature. My hope is that this book will give its readers some resources and ideas for participating in this urgent intellectual and political project.

–1–
Decolonization and Literature: A History

This chapter outlines the disciplinary history of English literature, setting the key ideas of postcolonial literary studies alongside other critical histories of the discipline. It begins with a summary of English literature's imperial-nationalist origins, drawing on accounts by Gauri Viswanathan and Terry Eagleton. It then offers a brief overview of the contributions of the figures who are most closely associated with the early years of postcolonial studies – Edward Said, Gayatri Chakravorty Spivak, and Homi Bhabha – as well as subsequent developments and critiques. Alongside this institutional history, the chapter introduces landmark interventions in the decolonization of literary studies by the explicitly anticolonial theorists Aimé Césaire, Frantz Fanon, Ngũgĩ wa Thiong'o, and Barbara Harlow. It focuses on the ways in which these thinkers help conceive the inseparability of what and how we read, as well as their claims for how literature can help us to imagine a decolonized future.

English literature's imperial history

The history of the discipline of English literature cannot be studied in isolation from the history of the British empire.

Gauri Viswanathan, in her path-breaking book *Masks of Conquest* (first published 1989), makes this claim explicit. She contends that, rather than being exported from Britain to its colonies, in fact English literature was first institutionalized as an academic subject in nineteenth-century British colonial India, at a time when the literary curriculum in England was still focused on classical Greece and Rome (Viswanathan, 2014 [1989], p. 3). This development came about because British colonial administrators were deeply concerned about the prospect of rebellion by the colonized Indian population, and they saw literature as a means of imaginative and social control that was more effective than direct military force (ibid., pp. 10–11). By presenting English literature as a superior source of knowledge, civilization, and authority, the British colonial education system not only construed Indian culture and knowledge as inferior; it also masked the 'sordid history' of British colonial rule, transforming the imagined figure of the Englishman from 'the rapacious, exploitative, and ruthless actor of history into the reflective subject of literature' (ibid., pp. 20–1). When English literature subsequently became established as a discipline in Britain, it similarly masked the violent and unequal incorporation of Scotland, Wales, and Ireland (later Northern Ireland) within the United Kingdom and promoted the idea of Britain as an imperial nation. As Michael Gardiner has argued, in the absence of a formal UK constitution, English literature was 'charged with the ideological task of describing a common ground for the "nation", understood in terms of ethnicity and empire' (2013, p. 2; see also Court, 1992, p. 14). The discipline bolstered the equation of Englishness with whiteness; erased Britain's own cultural heterogeneity and multi-national character; and obscured English literature's interdependence and exchange with literatures from across the world, including the rest of Europe and the British colonies.

Even if English literature instruction was not as homogeneous or effective in disseminating these ideologies as some of its practitioners imagined (cf. Court, 1992, pp. 14–15; Graff, 2007, pp. 12–13; Knights, 2017, p. 35), the discipline cannot

Decolonization and Literature   13

be divorced from this history. Even today, ideas of British sovereignty and cultural superiority continue to influence English literary education, at both school and university. For example, at the time of writing, UK government guidance for the General Certificate of Secondary Education (GCSE) English Literature examination – which is compulsory for the majority of secondary school students in England, Wales, and Northern Ireland – requires that students learn to 'appreciate the depth and power of the English literary heritage' (AQA Education, 2021, p. 15). Preparation for the exam must include Shakespeare, a '19th century novel', and one of twelve set works of modern drama and prose (the current list includes only two texts by British writers of colour, Kazuo Ishiguro and Meera Syal). Students' literary education is thus restricted to texts written in English in Britain and to a particular list of canonized writers and forms, described as 'the best that has been thought and written' (ibid., p. 15). There is no requirement that students read texts by Black or other authors of colour or from the rest of the world (cf. Sundorph, 2020), and no justification is given for the selection of these particular texts; the idea of 'English literary heritage' is presented as self-explanatory.

The discipline's imperial legacy also persists in less obvious ways. For instance, a longstanding principle of English literary studies is the notion of aesthetic autonomy, which can be summarized as the idea that the formal and stylistic qualities of a work reflect the artistic innovations of its creator, rather than the historical context in which it was produced or the author's own background or politics. This idea remains so ingrained in the discipline (despite repeated challenges from Marxist, historicist, and postcolonial critics) that it seems like common sense to many readers. However, in his 1983 work *Literary Theory: An Introduction*, Terry Eagleton argues that the idea of aesthetic autonomy has a history: it can be traced to the eighteenth-century British Romantics' critical response to the rise of industrial capitalism, which was made possible by Britain's appropriation of raw materials and cheap labour – including enslaved labour – from its colonies. The Romantics presented the creative imagination as a form

14 Decolonization and Literature

of resistance to the utilitarianism of the market and art as a radical political force. Yet, by emphasizing art's autonomy from market forces, the Romantics perhaps inadvertently facilitated the idea of a divide between aesthetics and politics, relinquishing the social role of art in favour of the notion of the freedom of the imagination. The association of art with individual freedom and creativity gained ground in the nineteenth and early twentieth centuries. In literary studies and popular literary culture, this gave rise to the idea that literature is an expression of 'universal' human values (narrowly imagined) rather than being profoundly entwined with the historical and political circumstances in which it is written (Eagleton, 1996, pp. 16–23).

The English literary canon that is outlined in the British GCSE curriculum, and that still comprises the 'core' curriculum in some university English literature departments, is underpinned by these contradictory claims to national representativeness *and* universal relevance. (Readers are encouraged to engage further with the idea of the canon in chapter 2.) The curriculum established by F. R. and Q. D. Leavis at the University of Cambridge in the 1930s includes names that remain familiar to many English literature students: Chaucer, Shakespeare, Blake, Wordsworth, Keats, Austen, Henry James, T. S. Eliot, D. H. Lawrence. The Leavises saw these figures as essentially English writers (even though James and Eliot grew up in the United States) whose work was also universally significant, because it transmitted a 'sensibility' that represented the highest expression of human ingenuity and artistic freedom (Eagleton, 1996, pp. 28–32).

It would be bad enough if this depoliticized and parochial understanding of what counts as good literature were restricted to literary education in Britain. But, as Ngũgĩ wa Thiong'o points out in his account of university literature education in post-Second World War Kenya, the colonial education system promoted this narrow view far more widely:

> These writers, who had the sharpest and most penetrating observations on the European bourgeois culture, were often taught as if their only concern was

Decolonization and Literature   15

with the universal themes of love, fear, birth and death.
Sometimes their greatness was presented as one more
English gift to the world alongside the bible and the
needle. ... The 'Great Tradition' of English literature
was the great tradition of 'literature'! (Ngũgĩ, 1986,
p. 91)

Ngũgĩ's critique recalls and extends Viswanathan's history
of the discipline. If English literature was first developed as
an academic subject to maintain social control in nineteenth-
century colonial India, it was then exported to educational
settings in other British colonies to play a similar role, and
it persisted in this role even after British imperialism had
formally ended.

Ngũgĩ is not suggesting that Kenyan readers have no use
for Chaucer and Eliot; rather, he is making the point that
these writers emerged from a particular historical context
and should be read accordingly. Part of that context is their
use within Britain's imperial apparatus. As Viswanathan
puts it:

I am not advocating that today's students must close
their English books without further ado because those
works were instrumental in holding others in subjugation ... [However,] we can no longer afford to regard
the uses to which texts were put in the service of British
imperialism as extraneous to the ways these texts are to
be read. (2014, p. 169)

The decolonization of literary studies must include a full
awareness and reckoning with this disciplinary history. This
does not mean that we should stop reading texts from the
traditional English (or European) canon altogether, not least
because to do so would mean skipping over a crucial stage
of the work of decolonizing. But we must situate these texts
in relation to their historical contexts and not automatically
privilege them over other texts in judgements of value or
importance. Decolonizing our discipline also requires that
we challenge our assumptions about what makes a work of

16 Decolonization and Literature

literature 'great' and familiarize ourselves with a wide range of literary traditions and approaches to literary criticism.

Summary

- The discipline of English literature was part of the British imperial effort to ensure social control and political hegemony in the colonies and Britain itself in the nineteenth and twentieth centuries (Viswanathan, 2014; Gardiner, 2013).
- The texts that make up the traditional English literary canon, as well as conventional critical approaches to these works, continue to influence the way that literature is studied in many schools and universities. For instance, the notion of 'English literary heritage' and the idea of aesthetic autonomy (Eagleton, 1996) are bound up in English literature's imperial history.
- The impact of the British colonial education system persisted even after the formal end of British colonialism, when the English literary canon continued to be taught as the sum total of 'great literature' (Ngũgĩ, 1986).
- A commitment to decolonizing literary studies does not mean that we must stop reading the English literary canon. However, it does mean that we must read canonical texts in relation to their use in the service of British imperialism, and also that we read widely in other literary and critical traditions.

Postcolonial literary studies

The scholarship I have been discussing was first published in the 1980s, when postcolonial studies was just starting to gain a foothold in English literature departments. As I observed in the Introduction, the emergence of this field has had a significant impact on the way that literature is studied and taught, especially in metropolitan anglophone universities

Decolonization and Literature 17

but also in schools and universities across the world. Much of what Viswanathan, Eagleton, and Ngũgĩ argue no longer seems controversial to most literature students and scholars. Writers such as Jane Austen and Charles Dickens are regularly read in relation to the history of slavery, colonial settlement, and imperial ideology, and courses in postcolonial or world literature, though not always compulsory, are part of nearly every undergraduate literature curriculum, not only in English departments but also in French and other historically European literature programmes. The history of this field should therefore be understood as an important, if incomplete, effort to decolonize literary studies.

The three scholars that are most closely associated with the rise of postcolonial literary studies are Edward Said, Gayatri Chakravorty Spivak, and Homi Bhabha. These figures share a number of biographical details: they were born in former British colonies (in Jerusalem, Calcutta, and Bombay, respectively) in the 1930s and 1940s; they spent most of their careers in prestigious literature departments in the United States (Said died in 2003, but at the time of writing Spivak and Bhabha still teach at Columbia and Harvard, respectively); and they wrote from the 1970s onwards about literary criticism's shortcomings and blind spots in relation to the history of empire. However, while the work of these three figures has indisputably been extremely influential in this field, there are some significant differences between their interventions.

Edward Said's *Orientalism* (1978) is often named as the founding text of postcolonial studies. The book argues that travel writing and scholarship by eighteenth- and nineteenth-century British and French writers played a crucial role in imagining what Said calls the 'Orient' – by which he means primarily the Middle East and North Africa – as a fitting site for European political and military domination. To conceive of the relationship between imperial governance and literature, he coins the term 'Orientalism', which he defines as (1) a field of academic study, comprising '[a]nyone who teaches, writes about, or researches the Orient'; (2) 'a style of thought' premised on a 'basic distinction between

East and West'; and (3) a 'corporate institution ... for dominating, restructuring, and having authority over the Orient' (1978, pp. 2–3). Said presents these three definitions of Orientalism as connected and interdependent. Drawing on Michel Foucault's concept of discourse, he argues that the production of literary and academic knowledge about the imagined 'Orient' was essential to British and French imperial rule, because it justified and naturalized the idea that the 'West' should dominate the 'East'.

It may now seem hard to imagine, but Said was one of the first critics to point out that the British and French literary canons of the eighteenth and nineteenth centuries were so closely linked to the history of empire. *Orientalism* also popularized the idea that Orientalist or Eurocentric representation produces its own reality, meaning that Europeans' misrepresentations of the 'Orient' came to replace the actual material reality of the region in the metropolitan imagination (Lazarus, 2004, p. 10). Said thus laid the ground for one of postcolonial studies' most important claims: namely, that the power struggle of the colonial encounter is carried out not only in the political and economic realms but also in the realm of culture (Elmarsafy et al., 2013, pp. 1–2). *Orientalism* has inspired countless studies of colonial representations of colonized places and people in literature and other art forms. It has also motivated many scholars to address the question that Said admits *Orientalism* does not answer: 'how one can study other cultures and peoples from a libertarian, or a nonrepressive and nonmanipulative, perspective' (Said, 1978, p. 24). (Said would go on to address the relationship between metropolitan and non-metropolitan responses to empire in his 1993 work *Culture and Imperialism*, which I discuss in chapter 4.) The question of how to study 'other cultures and peoples' in an ethical and emancipatory way is a key preoccupation for postcolonial literature scholars based in Western European and North American universities, who themselves have been accused of neo-Orientalism for producing knowledge about 'others' that in fact benefits primarily their own careers and institutions (Spivak, 2009 [1993], pp. 312–13; Boehmer, 1998).

Decolonization and Literature

Gayatri Chakravorty Spivak's body of writing in the 1980s – particularly 'Three women's texts and a critique of imperialism' (1985), *In Other Worlds* (1987), and 'Can the subaltern speak?' (1988 [1985]) – is also deeply concerned with the problem of representation as a means of imperial domination. Rather than taking Said's historicist approach to the colonial literary archive, however, Spivak deploys the strategy of deconstruction of the French-Algerian philosopher Jacques Derrida, which seeks to expose the instability of any meaning conveyed by language. Spivak uses deconstruction to analyse a wide range of topics, including Third World women's political movements, the history and politics of Third World development, and postcolonial literature, most notably the work of the Bengali writer Mahasweta Devi (Morton, 2002, pp. 25–7). Dismissing the charge that deconstruction is politically ineffective, Spivak uses it to highlight the ways in which dispossessed and marginalized people, particularly South Asian women, have been silenced by those who claim to speak as their representatives.

To give the best-known example of this argument: at the end of her essay 'Can the subaltern speak?', Spivak introduces the story of Bhuvaneswari Bhaduri, a young middle-class woman who committed suicide in her father's apartment in Calcutta in 1926. Although the suicide was staged as an act of *sati* (widow suicide), Bhuvaneswari was not married, and it later emerged that she had been involved in the armed struggle for Indian independence. Spivak presents her story as 'an unemphatic, ad hoc, subaltern rewriting of the text of *sati*-suicide', which provides a glimpse of Bhuvaneswari's own voice and agency that cannot be fully explained by nationalist or patriarchal paradigms: 'The subaltern as female cannot be heard or read' (Spivak, 1988, pp. 103–4). By naming Bhuvaneswari as subaltern (meaning marginalized) because of her gender, Spivak's feminist critique points to the erasure of her experience within a male-dominated narrative of anticolonial resistance. Spivak refuses to offer a better way of representing Bhuvaneswari instead; her point is that all political and academic representation under capitalist imperialism silences the disempowered, because the dominant

20 Decolonization and Literature

terms of representation do not allow individuals to speak for themselves in any context in which they are positioned as subaltern (Lazarus, 2004, p. 9). She is therefore more pessimistic than Said about the possibility of studying others in a non-repressive way and thus, as her later work states more explicitly, more sceptical about the political and intellectual value of metropolitan postcolonial studies.

Homi Bhabha is also influenced by Foucault and Derrida's emphasis on discourse and representation, but he is more hopeful than Spivak about the possibilities of discursive resistance. His book *The Location of Culture* (1994), a collection of influential essays first published in the 1980s and early 1990s, is best known for introducing the concepts of hybridity, mimicry, difference, and ambivalence to postcolonial studies. These terms describe the ways in which colonized people's everyday acts undermine and resist colonial power, which Bhabha argues is never as secure or total as it appears (Huddart, 2006, p. 1). It is important to note that, after this intervention, Bhabha did not publish any other significant scholarship in postcolonial studies. This distances him from Said and Spivak, whose contributions span several decades and have been more broadly influential in this and many other fields. However, I include Bhabha here because of the widespread and lasting impact of his ideas in postcolonial literary criticism, especially during the field's heyday in the 1990s and 2000s.

Bhabha draws substantially on psychoanalytic theory for his arguments, particularly the work of Freud and Lacan. For example, he contends that the unconscious profoundly influences the formation of identity and agency in colonial contexts. Although the colonial authority wants to posit an absolute difference between colonizer and colonized, they unconsciously know that this opposition cannot be sustained, and the colonized subject can exploit the anxiety that this knowledge produces (Huddart, 2006, pp. 3–4, 44–6; Moore-Gilbert, 2000, pp. 457–9). Bhabha thus rejects the idea of an inherently antagonistic relationship between these two positions, seeing the colonial relationship as interdependent: 'It is not the colonialist Self or the colonized Other, but the

Decolonization and Literature 21

disturbing distance in-between that constitutes the figure of colonial otherness – the white man's artifice inscribed on the black man's body. It is in relation to this impossible object that the liminal problem of colonial identity and its vicissitudes emerges' (2004 [1994], p. 64). As Bart Moore-Gilbert points out (2000, p. 459), Bhabha does not offer empirical evidence for such claims: they are based on his readings of texts by writers from both sides of the colonial divide, including John Stuart Mill, Joseph Conrad, Rudyard Kipling, Frantz Fanon, Salman Rushdie, and V. S. Naipaul. Crucially (and unlike Spivak, who identifies as a Marxist), Bhabha is hostile to the Marxist tradition: he rejects systematic analysis in favour of a lens of 'complexity' and privileges the experiential conditions of migrancy, liminality, and hybridity over struggle-based forms of politics (Lazarus, 2004, p. 4; Moore-Gilbert, 2000, p. 462).

The combined impact of these interventions on literary studies has been immense. After Said, Spivak, and Bhabha, it became common to situate literary texts in relation to the history of European colonialism and its aftermath and to read them in terms of their efforts to justify, suppress, or resist various forms of colonial and neocolonial oppression. A selection of texts by anglophone writers from former British colonies in Africa, South Asia, and the Caribbean – such as Chinua Achebe, Wole Soyinka, Ngũgĩ wa Thiong'o, Salman Rushdie, and Derek Walcott – became standard inclusions in university English literature courses and frequent subjects of scholarly analysis. Meanwhile, the growing consensus that postcolonial literary studies had become a field in its own right gave rise to a huge outpouring of scholarship that sought to define or contest its parameters and approach (e.g. Ashcroft et al., 2002 [1989]; Boehmer, 1995; Loomba, 1998; Young, 2001, 2020 [2003]; Lazarus, 2004; Huggan, 2013).

However, the considerable differences between Said, Spivak, and Bhabha's arguments make it hard to see how their work constitutes a field or method. One important difference is that, while all three scholars seek to demonstrate European writers' complicity in colonial domination, Said insists that the reason colonial fantasies about the 'Orient'

22   Decolonization and Literature

matter is that such ideas legitimized and maintained colonial systems of governance. Spivak and Bhabha, by contrast, focus on the violence of representation and the possibility of individual resistance to it and have less to say about literature's relationship to systems and institutions of imperial violence and dispossession. Benita Parry, in one of the most trenchant of the 'materialist' critiques of Spivak and Bhabha, notes that they cannot be accused of political quietism, since each proposes a politics of reading. However, she contends that, by denying the colonized subject any ground from which to respond to imperial aggression (Spivak), rejecting the idea of the colonizer and colonized as antagonists (Bhabha), and disparaging the struggles of the anticolonial national liberation movements (both), Spivak and Bhabha 'obliterat[e] the role of the native as historical subject and combatant' (1987, pp. 32–5, 36, 42; cf. Parry, 2004).

For me, this is the most troubling aspect of the poststructuralist strand of postcolonial literary studies that took inspiration from Spivak's early work and Bhabha's essays, and that was dominant during the field's peak. Much of this scholarship privileged post-independence texts that expressed disillusionment about the outcomes of the mid-twentieth-century anticolonial liberation movements, while engaging comparatively little with the literature and theory that came out of the movements themselves. Thus, as Jennifer Wenzel (2017) points out, the problem with understanding postcolonial studies as a continuation of 'the struggle for decolonization by other means' is that it stands 'in ambivalent or even somewhat antagonistic relation' to those earlier struggles. She agrees with Neil Lazarus that the field should instead be understood as 'a rationalization of and pragmatic adjustment to, if not quite a celebration of, the downturn in the fortunes and influence' of national liberationism and revolutionary socialism from the 1970s onwards (Lazarus, 2004, p. 5). Because poststructuralist postcolonial studies understood those battles as lost and disavowed the political affiliations of their participants, it overlooked 'the radical *theorizing* of decolonization' that the anticolonial national liberation movements produced (Wenzel, 2017).

The current turn from postcolonial to world literature raises additional problems. This turn represents a salutary move away from the anglophone canon that has dominated postcolonial literary studies, since the category of 'world literature' expressly includes texts in other European and non-European languages (often in translation, but also in the original) and from Latin America and the Middle East/North Africa. However, it risks shifting our attention even further from the history and practice of decolonization, since it removes the historical and political rationale for reading texts from former European colonies alongside one another. Moreover, as Aamir Mufti argues, the idea of world literature itself has a colonial genealogy, since it emerges from eighteenth- and nineteenth-century Orientalist philology, the same scholarship that Said identified as providing moral and intellectual ballast for the British and French empires. Mufti observes that Johann Wolfgang von Goethe's oft-cited concept of *Weltliteratur* seeks to assimilate 'Eastern' literature (represented by a Chinese 'novel') into the European 'universal' library. Mufti suggests that the same system of cultural mapping and assimilation persists in contemporary theorizations of world literature by such major critics as Franco Moretti, Pascale Casanova, and David Damrosch, because they also present the world 'as an assemblage of civilizational entities' without sufficiently attending to the inequities between different sites of literary production (2016, pp. 3, 19–20). To put this critique into the terms of my Introduction, this understanding of world literature diversifies without decolonizing; it expands the breadth of what 'we' (metropolitans) read, but it doesn't change how we read it.

It is possible, however, to conceive of the world from the perspective of decolonization, as many of the participants in the mid-twentieth-century national liberation struggles did themselves, as part of their commitment to an anti-imperialist internationalism. Ben Etherington, in a discussion of the theorist and poet Aimé Césaire (to whom I will return shortly), argues that Césaire's vision of a universalism 'enriched by every particular' usefully reframes world literature as a way of conceiving the co-existence of specific local cultures, histories, and practices 'within the empire of capital, whether in its colonial or globalizing phase' (2018, p. 60). This is a very different idea of the universal from the British imperial-nationalist formulation criticized by Eagleton and Viswanathan, since it explicitly rejects the idea that British literature and culture are the standard to which all others should aspire. Importantly, for Césaire this kind of universalism could only be realized through formal decolonization: 'political sovereignty held the promise of recovering cultural particularities that had been suppressed under colonial rule' (ibid.). Literature was a key medium for this kind of collective cultural recovery and for the anticolonial movements' other ambitions: it sought to unite participants in the struggle, communicate principles and tactics to people within and outside the movement, and envision the better world to come after imperialism was defeated. Resistance did not take place within the text alone; the literature of decolonization pointed relentlessly beyond itself, to the organized resistance movements it aimed to foster and support.

Summary

- Although postcolonial literary studies has diversified the English and European literature canons and changed how these texts are read and taught, it represents an incomplete attempt to decolonize literary studies.
- Edward Said, Gayatri Chakravorty Spivak, and Homi Bhabha are considered to be the founding figures of this field. Despite a shared interest in imperial discourse and representation, there are significant differences between their interventions.
- Said's *Orientalism* (1978) argues that the production of literary and academic knowledge about the 'Orient' legitimized the imperialist belief that the

Decolonization and Literature 25

'West' should rule the 'East'. His argument underpins postcolonial studies' claim that the colonial contest occurs in the cultural as well as political and economic realms.

- Spivak (1985, 1987, 1988) uses Derridean deconstruction to highlight the ways in which subaltern (marginalized) people, particularly women, have been silenced by those who claim to represent them. She argues that there is no way for the subaltern to speak for themselves under capitalist imperialism.
- Bhabha (1994) uses psychoanalytic theory to argue for the interdependence of colonizer and colonized. He posits hybridity, mimicry, difference, and ambivalence as manifestations of the colonized subject's resistance to colonial power.
- The poststructuralist strand of postcolonial studies that was influenced by Spivak and Bhabha's work did not engage significantly with the texts that emerged from the mid-twentieth-century national liberation struggles. The turn to world literature moves still further from this archive. However, it is possible to conceive of world literature from the perspective of decolonization by considering the role that literature and culture has played in anticolonial movements.

Literature and decolonization

I argued in the last section that the efforts of postcolonial literary scholars to decolonize the wider discipline remain incomplete. A key task for literature students and scholars who wish to move this project forward is to redress literary studies' relative lack of attention to the literary and cultural theory that emerged from the mid-twentieth-century decolonization struggles. The thinkers whose work I will discuss are already prominent names in literary studies, but their contributions to how we think about aesthetics and form deserve more sustained and serious attention. Each of them offers ways of decolonizing the practice of literary criticism that help us to move beyond mere diversification of our reading lists and thus from what to how we read.

In order to make this shift, we must transform dominant understandings of 'literature' and 'the literary'. As I have already suggested, literary studies depends on a narrow definition of what counts as 'good' literature, one that postcolonial studies has not substantially challenged or dislodged. Instead, certain kinds of formal experimentation – irony, metafiction, fragmentation, generic instability – have been recognized as characteristically postcolonial, a perception that disregards a much wider range and variety of literary production from the former colonies and metropolitan centres. These preferences might be attributed to the selection of writers such as Salman Rushdie as exemplary, which is partly a result of Bhabha's influence (McLeod, 2013, pp. 450, 455–8). However, it also stems from what Timothy Brennan has called the 'modernist literary dominant' (2017, p. 267) of the discipline of literary studies as a whole, which favours writers influenced by modernism and postmodernism and rejects works that are seen to be 'didactic'. Yet as Brennan counters, realism, reportage, earnestness, and exhortation are also forms of literary experimentation, as well as common features of peripheral (meaning non-metropolitan) aesthetics (ibid., pp. 269–75; cf. Brennan, 2014; Lazarus, 2011). While our critical vocabulary for analysing such texts remains limited, we don't have to start from scratch. There is a large body of work belonging to what Brennan calls the 'civic tradition', much of it emerging from decolonization struggles, that offers plenty of inspiration for thinking about the relationship between political argument and literary form.

Aimé Césaire, who was mentioned at the end of the previous section, was from Martinique, a Caribbean island and former French colony that remains a semi-autonomous French territory. His manifesto *Discours sur le colonialisme* (*Discourse on Colonialism*) was first published by the Paris

Decolonization and Literature 27

publishing house Présence Africaine in 1955. More than two decades before Said's *Orientalism*, the book anticipates Said's argument that European literature is profoundly invested in the legitimization and maintenance of empire. Césaire, too, quotes extensively from colonial documents, literature, and scholarship, exposing the overt racism within supposedly 'disinterested' academic knowledge (2000 [1955], p. 62). However, Césaire presents these arguments in a very different style from Said. He is explicit about his anti-imperialist and anti-capitalist politics, and his argument depends as much on its register as its content. Césaire moves between rage, lament, and invective, at one point comparing the racist statements of the poet Jules Romains on Black people's intellect to 'the braying of a Missouri ass' (ibid., p. 51). He counters the lies of the colonial archive with an account of colonialism's real costs:

> They talk to me about progress, about 'achievements,' diseases cured, improved standards of living.
> *I* am talking about societies drained of their essence, cultures trampled underfoot, institutions undermined, lands confiscated, religions smashed, magnificent artistic creations destroyed, extraordinary *possibilities* wiped out. (Ibid., pp. 42–3)

Although Césaire does not make specific suggestions about how authors or critics should respond to this history, the text itself is its own example. It is not possible simply to summarize Césaire's main ideas and still convey *Discourse*'s impact: the fury and virtuosity of his prose are part of his argument. For instance, Césaire highlights the written text's ability to mimic the properties of speech by making frequent use of anaphora (the repetition of a word or phrase at the beginning of successive clauses). In the passage just cited, he goes on to repeat the phrase '*I* am talking about' (*je parle de*) four more times, following each iteration with another impassioned statement of the colossal scale of colonial devastation. This technique makes the text seem more like a political speech at a demonstration, summoning the sense of collective energy and purpose that characterizes such events. It upends any association of didacticism with boredom, exhorting the reader to join in its revolt not only because of the persuasiveness of its case but through sheer exuberance.

The theorist and psychiatrist Frantz Fanon was also from Martinique, and at one point was Césaire's student. He later moved to Algeria and became a member of the Front de Libération Nationale (National Liberation Front, FLN) fighting for Algeria's independence from France; much of his work comes out of his experience within this movement. Fanon's contribution to the theorization of decolonization is immense and cannot be done justice here (see, among others, Alessandrini, 2014; Etherington, 2016; Fanon, 2018; Macey, 2012). However, his essay 'On National Culture' (1959, originally delivered as a speech to the Congress of Black Writers and Artists and published in *The Wretched of the Earth* [1963] after Fanon's untimely death in 1961) is relevant to my discussion because it makes a case for the kind of literature that is required to overcome colonialism's political and cultural legacy. The key contribution of 'On National Culture' is its delineation of three stages of cultural resistance to empire. In the first stage, 'assimilation', the 'native intellectual', meaning a member of the educated colonized elite, imitates European literary forms and styles to prove that he has mastered colonial culture. (My summary preserves Fanon's original use of masculine pronouns.) In the second stage, 'immersion', the intellectual rejects European precedents and looks to pre-colonial culture for inspiration. This is a not so subtle reference to the Négritude movement, which was very influential in francophone African literature and beyond in the 1930s and 1940s (see Rebaka, 2015). However, Fanon argues that this phase shows the intellectual's alienation from his native culture rather than his knowledge of it: he is stuck in the pre-colonial past rather than thinking about the postcolonial future. Finally, in the third stage, the work of literature and culture joins with the project of popular anticolonial revolution, and the native intellectual 'turns himself into an awakener of the people;

Decolonization and Literature   29

hence comes a fighting literature, a revolutionary literature, and a national literature' (Fanon, 1963, p. 223). The idea of 'national culture' belongs to this final stage. National culture is not focused on the past. It is proleptic, which means that it anticipates and seeks to bring about a more equal future after colonialism. National culture does not precede the struggle against colonialism; it is made in the course of that struggle and cannot be separated from it.

Fanon's idea of national culture posits the struggle against colonial rule as the primary horizon of interpretation for texts emerging from such movements. It encourages us to prioritize in our readings the creativity and courage of these texts' political imaginations rather than a separate set of aesthetic criteria. While this can be criticized as a 'doctrinaire' idea of culture (Etherington, 2016, p. 176), it usefully challenges the 'modernist literary dominant' (Brennan, 2017, p. 267) by making us think about what it would mean to see literature's contribution to political struggle as its most important attribute. This means not that a text has to espouse a certain 'correct' politics but that it seeks first and foremost to contribute, in both its content and its form, to the debates and challenges of a particular struggle (Harlow, 1987, pp. 29–30).

Ngũgĩ wa Thiong'o, the Kenyan novelist and literary critic already cited above, makes a concrete suggestion about how to produce such a 'national culture' in his 1986 work *Decolonising the Mind*: he demands that African writers stop writing in European languages. Indeed, he identifies *Decolonising the Mind* as his own 'farewell to English' (1986, p. xiv), stating that, going forward, he will write only in his native language, Gĩkũyũ. (I return to Ngũgĩ's intervention in my discussion of the language politics of 'English' literature in chapter 3.) Ngũgĩ sees the persistence of African literature in European languages as a sign of 'the psychological violence' inflicted in colonial schools like the one he attended, where students were punished for speaking Gĩkũyũ and rewarded for achievement in English (ibid., pp. 9–12). It also indicates the social and political dominance of the national bourgeoisie that produced most of

30 Decolonization and Literature

this literature: this class assumed power after independence and betrayed the anticolonial struggle by allowing the former imperial powers to maintain neocolonial economic control. In response, African literature in European languages 'became more and more critical, cynical, disillusioned ... It was almost unanimous in its portrayal ... of the post-independence betrayal of hope' (ibid., p. 21). (This is a body of writing that has been prominent in postcolonial literary studies, as I noted earlier.)

However, Ngũgĩ contends that, throughout this period, pre-colonial African languages 'were kept alive by the peasantry' and the working class (1986, p. 23). To choose to write in one of these languages is therefore to declare one's alliance with these classes instead of the bourgeoisie. Ngũgĩ also sees language as a means of transmitting the specific worldview of a culture, which is conveyed not 'through language in its universality but in its particularity as the language of a specific community with a specific history' (ibid., p. 15), a formulation that echoes Césaire's previously discussed notion of a universalism made up of particulars. However, Ngũgĩ notes that the choice of language is only a first step: literature must also 'carry the content of our people's anti-imperialist struggles to liberate their productive forces from foreign control' and 'create a higher system of democracy and socialism in alliance with all the other peoples in the world' (ibid., pp. 29–30). Ngũgĩ thus confirms Fanon's emphasis on the contribution that literature makes to an ongoing national and international struggle but adds the consideration of language to Fanon's discussion of content and form.

A final contribution to mention here comes from Barbara Harlow. While Harlow's background as a white academic from the United States is different from that of the other figures I have been discussing, her 1987 work *Resistance Literature* is a monumental effort to synthesize the literary and theoretical corpus of the mid-twentieth-century decolonization struggles and make it known to anglophone readers. Harlow's book appeared at the same time as other early texts in US postcolonial literary studies

Decolonization and Literature   31

– it came out the year before the most widely read version of Spivak's 'Can the Subaltern Speak?', for instance – but it has a very different emphasis. Harlow takes inspiration from the term 'resistance literature' (*al-adab al-muqawama*) coined by the Palestinian novelist and theorist Ghassan Kanafani. As Harlow explains, Kanafani used the term to describe texts that sought to contribute to the burgeoning Palestinian national liberation movement (Harlow, 1987, p. 2; Kanafani, 1968), again recalling Fanon's definition of national culture. Harlow broadens Kanafani's definition to include all literature produced by '[t]he struggle for national liberation and independence ... [including] literary writing, both narrative and poetic, as well as a broad spectrum of theoretical analyses of the political, ideological, and cultural parameters of this struggle' (Harlow, 1987, p. xvi). The book foregrounds texts from Palestine, Nicaragua, and apartheid South Africa, struggles that were all then still ongoing. It also draws on theoretical work by Ngũgĩ, Fanon, Abdelfatah Kilito, Amílcar Cabral, José Carlos Mariátegui, and many other participants in decolonization struggles. Harlow draws anglophone readers' attention to this neglected archive as a demonstration of the key role that cultural resistance played within these movements. Unlike in 'Western' literature and literary criticism, Harlow argues, 'the emphasis in the literature of resistance is on the political as the power to change the world. The theory of resistance literature is in its politics' (ibid., p. 30). It must be emphasized that Harlow is not using the term 'resistance' to refer to all forms of opposition or defiance: she is referring specifically to organized movements of resistance to colonial and semi-colonial rule.

In this rest of this book, I seek to build on the insights of these and many other thinkers who have been inspired by the key role that cultural production played in the mid-twentieth-century anticolonial liberation struggles. The next chapter takes these ideas to the classroom in order to begin thinking about how we can put the history and practice of decolonization at the heart of our work as literature students, teachers, and critics.

Decolonization and Literature

Summary

- Postcolonial literary studies has privileged a modernist and postmodernist aesthetics. The literature and theory of the mid-twentieth-century decolonization struggles challenges this narrow approach and advances our understanding of the relationship between political argument and literary form.
- Césaire's *Discourse on Colonialism* (1955) demonstrates the importance of form and style in putting forth anticolonial arguments through its use of emotional register, repetition, invective, and virtuosic prose.
- Fanon's 'On National Culture' (1959) defines national culture as a 'fighting' and 'revolutionary' literature that is made in the course of anticolonial struggle and seeks to envision and bring about a genuinely postcolonial future.
- Ngũgĩ's *Decolonising the Mind* (1986) identifies writers' choice of language as key to cultural decolonization, demanding that African writers ally themselves with the peasantry and working class and write in their indigenous languages instead of European imperial languages.
- Harlow's *Resistance Literature* (1987) synthesizes the literature and theory of the mid-twentieth-century decolonization struggles. Following the Palestinian novelist Ghassan Kanafani, she names this work as 'resistance literature', arguing that it should be interpreted and assessed in relation to its contribution to anticolonial resistance movements.

–2–
Unfinished Business: How Do We Decolonize Literature?

This chapter considers the task of decolonizing literary studies from the vantage point of the undergraduate classroom. Readers are encouraged to reflect on where their criteria for recognizing 'good' literature come from and how their study of literature has been organized. I offer a brief overview of current efforts to expand and diversify the literature curriculum beyond the traditional canon with reference to curricular trends in metropolitan anglophone universities and current editions of major teaching texts. Readers are then invited to consider how students and educators can move beyond mere diversification to tackle the problem of transforming *how* as well as *what* we read. This challenge requires us to address not only the content and structure of courses but also 'the tasks required to engage' with texts (Morreira and Luckett, 2018). My discussion draws on Ngũgĩ wa Thiong'o, Henry Owuor Anyumba, and Taban Lo Liyong's pathbreaking essay 'On the abolition of the English department' (1968); the 'Decolonising SOAS' toolkit (SOAS, 2018); and examples of efforts to develop strategies for reading poetics and politics together in my own and other colleagues' teaching and research. I also suggest some ways of discussing these topics in the classroom and invite readers to think about adaptations for their own geographical, linguistic, and institutional contexts.

Reflection I: Your literary education

1. How do you define a 'good' or 'classic' work of literature? Where does your definition come from?
2. What made you decide to study literature at university? What kinds of texts did you expect to read, and what did you want to read?
3. What texts would you name as belonging to 'the canon'? How do the conventional canons of English literature, European literature, and world literature differ, and where do they intersect or overlap? Are there texts that all three canons include?
4. What texts, writers, genres, periods, and/or approaches have you found yourself most drawn to during your studies? Why do you think that is?
5. What backgrounds have your teachers come from (race/ethnicity, gender, nationality, class, etc.)? Have they discussed their own backgrounds in relation to the texts you've studied together and/or encouraged you to reflect on yours?

The changing canon and its limits

In her closing reflections on the history of English literature studies in British colonial India, Gauri Viswanathan argues that, in order to understand the process of canon formation, the curriculum must be 'studied less as a receptacle of texts than as activity, that is to say, as a vehicle of acquiring and exercising power' (2014, p. 167). The canon of English literature, like that of literature in other languages, has never been a fixed list of titles: what we consider to be 'classic' or 'canonical' literature at a certain place and time registers the victories and compromises of struggles for control within departments and disciplinary associations, across institutions, and in culture and society at large. Debates over which texts literature students should study have been present since the beginning of the profession (Graff, 2007, pp. 2–3) and have often reflected wider cultural trends and disputes. To offer a famous example: during the US 'culture wars' of the 1980s and 1990s, right-wing media commentators denounced efforts at Stanford and other elite US universities to include more women and writers of colour in the literature curriculum as an attack on 'American values' and 'western civilization' (Hartman, 2015, pp. 222–52; see also Alessandrini, 2023, chapter 2). Such claims persist in contemporary attacks on efforts to decolonize the curriculum. For instance, in response to the open letter from Cambridge University English literature students that I cited in my Introduction, the British *Daily Telegraph* ran a front-page story with the headline 'Student forces Cambridge to drop white authors'. It featured a full-page photo of the letter's lead author Lola Olufemi, who is Black; Olufemi was then subjected to an onslaught of racist and sexist abuse online. The *Telegraph* issued a correction two days later, admitting that the letter's 'proposals were in fact recommendations' (Ponsford, 2017; cf. Turner, 2017).

Such responses demonstrate the degree to which the idea of the 'English' or 'Western' canon remains fundamental to white supremacist discourse, as well as the formidable consequences for students or staff – particularly Black and other women of colour – who are perceived to threaten its dominance. However, as I noted in the last two chapters, over the last several decades scholars and students of postcolonial, feminist, and metropolitan ethnic minority literatures have brought about significant changes in the literature curriculum that most students in metropolitan anglophone universities now encounter. Even a cursory survey of module and course offerings in leading English literature departments in the US, the UK, and Australia reveals this shift towards diversification.[3] For instance, although most departments continue to organize their curriculum according to a conventional 'chronological spine' (Krishnan, 2019) from the medieval period to the present day, within this structure most programmes also offer a significant number of modules on texts by authors from under-represented and marginalized groups, including

Black American, Black British, women's, and queer writing, as well as modules on postcolonial or world literature. (There are still departments where options in these subject areas are reserved for the final year of the undergraduate degree and students must choose between them, but these departments are the exception.) Such modules tend to be available primarily in the post-1945 period, with some earlier period options on such topics as literature and colonialism or literature and slavery, although modules with broad earlier period titles such as 'Medieval Literature' or 'Early Modern Literature' also often attend to questions of race, gender, and conquest. Modules on writing by under-represented groups tend to be optional, although world literature courses are sometimes compulsory, and some US departments include a 'diversity' requirement. As I noted in the Introduction, modules that feature Black or Brown writers often privilege domestic ethnic minority writing: this trend is particularly noticeable in US English departments, where students can often choose from a range of modules on Black American, Asian-American, Latinx, and/or Indigenous American writing but have fewer opportunities to study writing from the rest of the world.

A comparable trend towards greater diversity on the basis of racial or ethnic identity can also be seen in the most recent editions of the influential *Norton Anthology of English Literature* (10th edn; Greenblatt, 2018) and *The Norton Anthology of Poetry* (6th edn; Ferguson et al., 2018). While the Norton anthologies have been accused of overlooking women and writers of colour (e.g. Shesgreen, 2009), the current editors have made an effort to broaden their scope.[4] For example, in the table of contents for Volume F (twentieth and twenty-first centuries) of *The Norton Anthology of English Literature*, there is a section on 'Nation, race, and language' comprised of poems and prose extracts by twelve Black and Brown writers, of whom six are from the Caribbean and five are Black women. Another eleven entries from Black and other writers of colour appear uncategorized in the remainder of the volume, all of them high-profile figures such as Salman Rushdie and Hanif Kureishi (who both also appear in the 'Nation, race, and language' section), Derek Walcott, Chinua Achebe, Zadie Smith, Chimamanda Adichie, and others. (As V. Nicholas LoLordo drily observes, when assessing the inclusivity of the contents tables of such anthologies, 'One may be tempted to count' [2004; see also Alessandrini, 2023, chapter 9].) *The Norton Anthology of Poetry*, which encompasses English-language poetry from the medieval period to the present, includes women poets in every historical period, among them the eighteenth-century Black American Phyllis Wheatley. In the twentieth and twenty-first century sections, more Black and other poets of colour appear, including writers from the Caribbean, South Asia, and Africa and from US ethnic minority backgrounds, such as Walcott, Lorna Goodison, Dom Moraes, Arthur Nortje, Agha Shahid Ali, Langston Hughes, N. Scott Momaday, Amiri Baraka, Louise Erdrich, Li-Young Lee, and Rita Dove. Similarly, the popular Cambridge Companions to Literature series, which was inaugurated in 1991 with volumes on Old English and Romanticism, has gradually expanded its purview. In 2004, the series published its first volume on Black writing, the *Cambridge Companion to African-American Literature*, as well as the *Cambridge Companion to Postcolonial Literary Studies*. At the time of writing, the series includes volumes on lesbian literature, Latin American poetry, James Baldwin, Rabindranath Tagore, and more, for a total of thirty-eight volumes (by my count) that focus on writing by people of colour, queer writing, or non-Euro/US texts in a list of 405 volumes, or a little under 10 per cent of the whole.

This is far from a sea change, but it is something more than the addition of a token text or topic area to a previous curriculum. Nation, race, gender, and sexuality are established topics of literary study, with a comparatively small but expanding group of associated authors that regularly appear on university reading lists. It is no longer accurate to describe the curriculum in most English literature departments as entirely 'male, pale, and stale'; significant inroads have been made, especially in the modern and contemporary periods. But it is also important to register the limits of these changes to the canon. Many English literature courses, like the Norton

38   Unfinished Business

anthologies, restrict themselves to texts written in English and do not address writing in translation, which necessarily limits their inclusiveness. (The profusion of world literature anthologies published since 2000 seeks to address this gap, though they do not have the same influence or reach as the English literature anthologies: see e.g. Damrosch and Pike, 2009; Puchner, 2018.) Meanwhile, the same Black and other writers of colour appear again and again; they are generally figures who are already widely recognized, either by literary prize culture (e.g. Tagore, Walcott, and Toni Morrison, all winners of the Nobel Prize for Literature) and/or the market (e.g. Smith and Adichie). Yet even these well-known writers are often treated as supplementary to the core programme of study. This can be seen in the 'Core Selections E-Book' version of the current edition of *The Norton Anthology of English Literature*, which is drawn from all six volumes of the anthology and contains only four Black and other writers of colour: the eighteenth-century author Olaudah Equiano and the contemporary bestselling novelists Smith, Adichie, and Kazuo Ishiguro.

To compound the problem of a limited selection of writers, the tendency to group texts by writers of colour together promotes the idea that these writers' racial, ethnic, or national identities determines what and how they write, while the same is not assumed to be true for white writers. In Volume F of *The Norton Anthology of English Literature*, half of the Black and Brown writers included in the volume are relegated to the section on nation, race, and language, foregrounding their biographies (and, in some cases, subject matter) at the expense of their form and style. Writers whose work can be read as 'voicing' the experience of a particular group are arguably also more likely to be taught or anthologized. For instance, LoLordo notes that the US ethnic minority poets who appear in *The Norton Anthology of Modern and Contemporary Poetry* (2003), co-edited by the Iranian-American postcolonial poetry scholar Jahan Ramazani, all work in a confessional and introspective mode. Their writing can thus be seen as providing 'unmediated access' to the experience of being Black or Indigenous

American or Latinx (LoLordo, 2004). This framing not only forecloses other ways of interpreting these writers' work; it also implicitly assumes a white reader who desires this kind of 'access' to the 'perspectives' of Black and Brown writers, positioning literary studies as 'a privileged tool that white [readers] can use to get to know difference' (Melamed, 2011, p. xvi). The problem with an emphasis on diversifying the curriculum, then, is that merely adding writers of colour (as well as women, queer, working-class, or disabled writers) to an otherwise unreconstructed curriculum guarantees that those writers will be seen as supplementary rather than essential and as emissaries of a particular group rather than creative practitioners in their own right. Decolonizing the curriculum, by contrast, requires us to rebuild our programmes of study from the ground up, decentring both the 'core' (western European and North American) curriculum and the presumptive white reader.

This is the kind of challenge to the status quo that Ngũgĩ wa Thiong'o and his University of Nairobi colleagues Henry Owuor Anyumba and Taban Lo Liyong present in their important 1968 essay 'On the abolition of the English department', which rejects a proposal to add a selection of African and other postcolonial writing in English to the department's existing curriculum. It is not enough, they write, to 'smuggle African writing into an English syllabus', as if Africa were merely 'an extension of the west' (Ngũgĩ et al., 1972 [1968], p. 146). Instead, they argue that the English department should be abolished, and a department of African literature and language set up in its place. English, French, and Swahili should be made compulsory, since the majority of African literature is written in those languages; African oral and written traditions should be given equal weight; and the study of language and linguistics should be required. Texts from the rest of the world should be included in the curriculum, but they 'are to be considered in their relevance to our situation, and their contribution towards understanding ourselves' (ibid., p. 146). Such a transformation has been blocked, they suggest, by a pernicious emphasis on 'literary excellence', which 'implies a value judgement as to

40   Unfinished Business

what is literary and what is excellence, and from whose point of view', at the expense of the study of 'representative works which mirror [local] society' (ibid., p. 149).

While the language of 'our situation' and 'ourselves' can degrade into a cultural nativism that is suspicious of migrants and minorities, I do not think that is what Ngũgĩ and his colleagues intend. They are speaking from a particular time and place, namely early post-independence Kenya, where the demand for cultural as well as political decolonization was particularly urgent (see also Helgesson, 2022, chapter 4). Their intervention resonates in other locations and in the present day because it demands that we reflect on how the literature curriculum is organized: which subjects are compulsory and which are optional, how artistic and intellectual value is assessed, and how disciplinary boundaries are constructed and maintained. Crucially, by identifying and questioning the assumptions that underpin the existing curriculum, they make it possible to imagine it differently. Indeed, they did more than imagine: today the Department of Literature at the University of Nairobi cites their essay as a foundational document on its website, and it offers programmes in oral literature, drama, literature and language, prose, and theatre and film studies, with an emphasis on Kenyan and other African writing and performance in each area.[5]

The insistence of Ngũgĩ and his colleagues that their department should put 'Kenya, East Africa, and then Africa in the centre' (1972, p. 146) prompts us to consider what it means to centre a university's geographical, cultural, and social location in its literature curriculum. What should the literature curriculum look like at a contemporary university in London, or the Palestinian West Bank, or West Bengal in India? What would it mean to prioritize works that 'mirror' these locations, in all their historical and social complexity? Who is the 'we' of a particular classroom or department? How should the 'relevance to our situation' of texts from the rest of the world be understood? How can we make an awareness of location and vantage point central to the teaching of our discipline? There are no simple or general answers to these questions, but the next section of this chapter suggests some ways that literature students and educators might develop our efforts to 'think from where we stand' (Krishnan, 2019).

Reflection II: The canon and the curriculum

1. Choose a recent anthology designed for use in the classroom (it could be a text discussed in this chapter, or one you've been assigned to read in class, or one you find in a library). Looking at the table of contents and other paratexts (editor's introduction, biographical notes for authors, etc.), try to determine the principles of canonization that are being employed. Which writers are included? How is their work introduced, presented, and organized? Are their backgrounds addressed, and, if so, is this the case for all writers in the collection or just those who are in some way marginalized? You may wish to compare examples of more and less 'diverse' collections.
2. Look at the lists of compulsory and optional modules for your literature degree or major. How is the programme structured? What kinds of topics or approaches are required, and which are optional or extra? What kinds of claims or assumptions about approaches to interpreting literary texts do the module titles and descriptions suggest?
3. What kind of 'ideal, imagined student' (Morreira and Luckett, 2018) does the literature curriculum in your department project? How do you think students from different backgrounds (race, gender, sexuality, religion, nationality, class, ability, etc.) experience this curriculum (Krishnan, 2019)?

Where do we go from here?

Current struggles to decolonize university curricula have generated a rich archive of manifestos and toolkits for transforming existing programme structures and syllabi. These documents often name the transformation of the curriculum as a first step in a wider struggle against systemic structures of exclusion and exploitation in universities, such as tuition fees, admissions and hiring practices, campus policing, institutional investment portfolios, and the use of low-paid, part-time teaching contracts (see also Jayawardane and Walcott, 2021). Many of these documents have emerged from collective conversations and campaigns taking place across universities, and thus they do not always offer recommendations for particular disciplines. However, they share a commitment to thinking from and across locations that is crucial to any effort to decolonize literary studies.

One notable example is the 'Decolonising SOAS: learning and teaching toolkit', published online by the Decolonising SOAS Working Group at SOAS University of London in 2018.[6] The toolkit defines decolonization as a practice that 'connects contemporary racialised disadvantages with historical processes of colonialism, [and] seeks to expose and transform them through forms of collective reflection and action' (SOAS, 2018, p. 3). It thus explicitly situates the decolonization of the curriculum as part of the fight against structural racism, indicating a relationship to wider social movements. The toolkit includes lists of questions to help instructors assess their own curriculum and pedagogy, such as whether their syllabus presumes a particular student and whether it takes in non-English-language and non-European sources; the transparency and accessibility of their teaching practice; their ability to recognize and address instances of racist behaviour in the classroom; and their success in training students to work with and challenge different points of view (ibid., pp. 9–10, 15–16). Its suggested adaptations offer ways to radically expand the knowledge base and types of sources that underpin the curriculum: instructors are encouraged to incorporate suggestions from students and from colleagues with different specializations, draw on material from journals located in the Global South, and historicize their discipline and teach its controversies. The document also prompts teachers to allow students to make connections to their existing knowledge and experiences (ibid., pp. 10, 16). These ideas point to two practices that are key to thinking from where we stand. They encourage teachers and students to treat their own knowledge and experience as a valid source of information, particularly if they come from backgrounds that are marginalized in their discipline and/or in British/anglophone public culture. However, educators and students from all backgrounds must also work to recognize 'the narrowness of their own frames of historical and epistemological reference' (Gopal, 2019, p. 79) and to extend and enhance their knowledge and understanding by critically engaging with texts from a wide range of contexts and standpoints.

Some of the reading list and course adaptations that the SOAS toolkit suggests can be made to existing literature syllabi and curricula fairly easily. Among these are reducing and decentring white metropolitan writers in secondary as well as primary reading lists, as well as making use of team teaching and student facilitation of class discussions to encourage breadth of study and comparative thinking. Another relatively simple change is to challenge the reliance on 'great books' by assigning lesser-known texts that widen the historical, geographical, thematic, and/or linguistic scope of the curriculum. Such interventions are made more difficult, unfortunately, by the economics of the publishing industry, which means that non-canonical texts and texts translated into English from other languages (especially non-European languages) are also less likely to remain in print or to be available in electronic form. I have frequently had to remove set texts from my own syllabi that sought to expand the module's outlook and scope because they were too hard for students to obtain or the university library was unable to legally digitize them, and I know that this is also true for many colleagues.

Other recommendations in the SOAS toolkit require more labour, organization, and collaboration between literature educators and students. As Ngũgĩ, Owuor Anyumba, and Liyong argue, decolonizing (or abolishing) the existing literature curriculum requires an overhaul of the content and structure of the course, with particular attention to the introductory and survey modules that present the subject matter, methods, and ideas of the discipline to new students. This is where an awareness of thinking from where we stand, both individually and collectively, becomes especially important. For instance, in a module such as 'Writing London' (a required first-year module in my London university's English Department), decolonizing the curriculum requires first of all that London's historical, cultural, linguistic, and ethnic parameters are expansively construed, foregrounding the city's imperial history, its history of migration, and its contemporary radical heterogeneity and inequality. In order to be able to situate a diverse range of London writing in a wider colonial, diasporic, and internationalist framework, however, students also need to study writing from the countries that were formerly ruled from London and to understand such texts as integral to their literary education, not supplemental or external to it. Of course, it is not possible to read all the world's literature in a lifetime, let alone in a three- or four-year undergraduate degree. However, it is possible to build a curriculum that encourages students to move between local, regional, international, and global frameworks and standpoints; to think about those standpoints critically and comparatively; and to conceive of literature as a key medium for connecting, interpreting, and inspiring different sites and epochs of struggle (cf. Forsdick, 2018, pp. 697–703, 708).

This approach to the curriculum requires instructors to help students develop strategies for reading politics and poetics together, and in relation to historical and contemporary social movements. I'll offer a few examples from my teaching and that of some of my colleagues to suggest different ways of responding to this challenge. My second-year undergraduate module 'Palestinian and Israeli Literature' (which is cross-listed in the English and Comparative Literature programmes) builds on my own experience of writing about texts from the region as a Palestine solidarity movement participant and US citizen of Jewish heritage who is neither Palestinian nor Israeli.

Although a small number of students begin the semester with a detailed knowledge of the history of the conflict and a developed political stance, many explain in our first conversations that they chose the module because they want more information about the region and its history. While I try to give them a narrative overview of the conflict – one that situates it in relation to the history of British imperialism and European Jewish settler-colonialism in British Mandate Palestine – I emphasize that the module is concerned with the specifically literary ways in which Palestinian and Israeli writers (read in translation) have responded to this history. The module presents the effort to read Palestinian- and Israeli-authored texts alongside one another not as a conciliatory activity or a production of 'dialogue' but, rather, as an acknowledgement that the two largely separate literary traditions are bound by a common historical situation (see also Bernard, 2013, pp. 7–14).

For the first class, I ask students to bring in an example of how the 'Israeli–Palestinian conflict' is represented internationally in the press or social media. This is intended to challenge the impression that this struggle is distant from their own lives, as well as to encourage them to recognize and respond critically to the racist and reductive tropes used to depict it. In the second class, we discuss the classic novella *Rijal fi al-shams* (1963; *Men in the Sun*, 1978), by the Palestinian novelist and Popular Front for the Liberation of Palestine (PFLP) party member Ghassan Kanafani, which was one of the first Palestinian literary texts published in English translation, following Kanafani's assassination in Beirut in 1972. We read the novella alongside an extract from Kanafani's essay 'Al-adab al-muqawama' ('Resistance literature', 1968), which I mentioned in chapter 1 in my discussion of Barbara Harlow's book *Resistance Literature*. I thus encourage students to approach Kanafani as a literary and political theorist whose fiction overtly seeks to contribute to the Palestinian national liberation struggle rather than as someone who simply 'reflects' or 'voices' Palestinian experience. To help students reach this conclusion themselves, I invite them to connect the main

46 Unfinished Business

points of Kanafani's argument to some of his key techniques in the novella, such as his use of characterization, interior monologue, and the scene, before opening the discussion to other kinds of response to his work. The use of a structured approach to the first part of the discussion aims to help students who might not yet feel confident about engaging with texts from this region to deploy the critical skills they already have. At the same time, it encourages participants to connect Kanafani's use of form and style to his commitment to building a Palestinian literature of resistance, which he described as a 'literature free of lamentation ... the poetry of resistance realizes its commitment to the revolutionary movement in the world, which is ultimately the climate in which the local revolutionary movement develops and grows' (Kanafani, 1968, p. 78).

Because the material covered on this module is politically controversial, there are challenges to teaching it beyond the effort to encourage students to consider its aesthetics along with its politics. While many students, including some who identify as Palestine solidarity activists, have told me that the encounter with texts written by Jewish-Israeli and Palestinian-Israeli authors has complicated their previous stereotypes about Israel, others have expressed concern with the module's pro-Palestine stance. One way that I have tried to engage with this response is by acknowledging my own background and standpoint at the start of the semester. I encourage students also to recognize their own standpoints and to disagree with me and with each other, as long as they do so in a respectful way and strive to consider other points of view. This effort has not always been successful – a student once wrote on a module evaluation form that I had said that I would only teach pro-Palestinian viewpoints, which is not what I said and not what the module does – but it speaks to some of the broader challenges of decolonizing the curriculum. Although the discourse about this project often pits recalcitrant, conservative academics against activist students, this is an oversimplification that overlooks the range of university students' political views, as well as the discomfort and resistance that students who feel themselves to be at odds with decolonizing initiatives may express. Other contentious issues such as transgender rights, refugee and migrant rights, Black and Indigenous struggles, anti-Muslim racism, and the topic of white supremacy itself present comparable challenges. Open discussion of texts that address such topics requires educators and students to engage seriously with the political questions they raise and to reflect honestly on our own commitments and affiliations in relation to contemporary struggles.

My colleague Amy De'Ath also seeks to give students tools to think about the relationship between literary form and political content and to challenge some of the assumptions they might hold about this relationship. She convenes an optional first-year undergraduate English module called 'Writing Race, Writing Gender' that invites students to question the conventional opposition between experimental writing and writing that emphasizes voice or identity. The module is team-taught, and De'Ath has asked all colleagues who contribute lectures to the module to introduce students to texts that can be characterized as experimental but are also centrally concerned with issues of race, gender, or class. In conversation with me, De'Ath explained that the module emerged from her desire to make the rarefied world of literature and literary criticism accessible to students and to help them feel confident reading 'difficult' material that doesn't immediately convey a message. At the same time, she wants to challenge students' tendency to approach poetry as a mode of self-expression, as well as the discipline's association of experimental writing of all kinds, but especially poetry, with white writers (De'Ath, 2020).

In her first lecture, De'Ath asks her audience to consider the terms 'avant-garde', 'difficult', and 'experimental'. She points out that these are all very loose terms that broadly privilege form over content but do not convey a particular list of characteristics.[7] What they share, however, is an assumption that such work is produced by white artists. As De'Ath puts it: 'this shift in the meaning of the "avant-garde", as it has come to connote more exclusively aesthetic properties – an emphasis on form as opposed to content, on abstraction, or the idea of a pure aestheticism itself – this has a racially-coded history.' As a result, critics who work on this material have not only neglected Black writing but have also assumed that writing that is explicitly concerned with racial identity is not avant-garde (De'Ath, 2019, citing Reed, 2014). De'Ath holds on to the term 'experimental' as an open-ended way of describing works that seek to redefine literary conventions, but she asks her listeners to consider which writers get to be experimental, who has access to their work, and where such work sits in relation to the literary marketplace. The lecture ends with a brief reading of the poem *S*PeRM**K*T* by the Black American poet Harryette Mullen (1992), in which De'Ath asks students to consider whether this 'difficult' poem can be said to be 'about' race and gender or not. The lecture thus calls students' attention to the structural racism of literary studies and literary publishing while encouraging them to question the assumptions and attitudes that underlie the techniques of poetic interpretation that they have been taught. It also introduces a set of questions to help students expand their definition of literary experimentation, which they can bring to bear on a wide range of texts. Finally, the lecture and the module seek to challenge the binary argumentation of the contemporary culture wars, which insists that one must either be for or against identity politics, by problematizing essentialist or static definitions of identity and asking students to think carefully about how group identities are formed and mobilized.

Heritage studies offers another point of entry into the contemporary culture wars and their relationship to literature. The example that follows comes from the UK, but the issues it raises are common to controversies over the social and educational role of museums and historical sites in other former imperial centres and settler-colonial countries such as France, the US, Canada, or Australia. In 2020, the National Trust, a publicly funded charity that maintains hundreds of historic buildings and land conservation sites across the UK, released an open-access online document entitled *Interim Report on the Connections between Colonialism and Properties now in the Care of the National Trust, including Links with Historic Slavery* (Huxtable et al., 2020). The report offers an overview of ongoing research into the connections of many of the Trust's properties with colonialism and slavery, focusing on the sources of wealth that funded these properties (ibid., pp. 5–6). Alongside the report, one of its editors, the literature and heritage scholar Corinne Fowler, ran a project called 'Colonial countryside' that invited primary school children to investigate connections to empire at selected National Trust properties and to present their findings to the public through exhibitions, child-led tours, creative writing, and classroom teaching materials (National Trust, n.d.). These initiatives enraged some Conservative members of the UK Parliament and right-wing media commentators, who accused the National Trust of 'wokery' and being 'overtaken' by Black Lives Matter activism (Doward, 2020).

This controversy reminds us once again of the powerful interests that efforts to decolonize the curriculum are up against, particularly when these efforts extend beyond the university classroom into primary and secondary education and the wider public sphere. For the politicians, columnists, and members of the public who railed against the National Trust report, any mention of the central role of colonialism and slavery in British history represented an attack on 'British values' and the British 'national character'. Reflecting on this response, Fowler observes that the 'determined opposition to an anti-colonial history suggests a nation at a crossroads, either prone to comforting nationalist myths' that occlude criticism of Britain's imperial past, or 'ready to embrace its fuller histories and the global connections of its people' (2021, p. 8; see also pp. 16–19). Fowler's recent scholarship (2021, 2023), which she calls 'purposely reparative' (2021, p. 7), contributes to this fuller history by juxtaposing discussion of these debates both with analysis of British Black and Asian writers' representations of the countryside and with her own creative and autobiographical responses to the histories her research on National Trust properties and British rural landscapes has uncovered. Similarly, Lucienne Loh's work on the 'postcolonial country' in the work of British Black and Asian writers highlights these writers' resistance to 'images of the English countryside as a stalwart metaphor for Englishness' and their challenge to the idea that multicultural life in Britain takes place only in cities (2013, p. 8).

Such scholarship offers an excellent starting point for addressing the question of British national identity and its relationship to empire with university students coming from a range of perspectives and backgrounds. Many students educated in the UK will have been taught almost nothing about Britain's colonial past (cf. Fowler, 2021, p. 17), and some will be reluctant to question the 'image of the placid, calm and idyllic English countryside, seat of tradition and history' (Loh, 2013, p. 25), that continues to underpin dominant ideas of Englishness and Britishness. Work such as Fowler's and Loh's exposes the historical role that British heritage institutions and British writers have played in promoting such ideas while also demonstrating the capacity of heritage work, literature, and literary criticism to challenge and undo them, both within and beyond the university classroom. Students might explore the historical archives that the *Interim Report* and the 'Colonial countryside' project draw on, such as the open-access database 'Legacies of British slavery' (Centre for the Study of the Legacies of British Slavery, 2022); write their own creative responses to these histories; or come up with their own ideas for conveying an anticolonial history of Britain to the public.

Finally, another colleague at my institution, Jonathan Ward, challenges the exclusionary setting of the university itself. His project 'The abolitionist curriculum' (Ward, 2020), to which several other colleagues have also contributed, is an online curriculum published on Wordpress that seeks to reach students who are not necessarily located in the undergraduate university classroom. Inspired by the Black feminist scholar bell hooks (1994) among others, the curriculum refuses the hierarchies that structure the university classroom as a space to which only some people have access, and where the instructor's knowledge and ideas are privileged over those of others in the room (Ward, 2021). The curriculum focuses on Black people's historical and ongoing resistance to oppressive institutions such as the transatlantic slave trade, apartheid, and the prison industrial complex. It also celebrates 'Blackness in all its abundant variations ... including Black joy, Black excellence, Black resistance, Black organizing, and Black love' (Ward, 2020). Among the recommended works are creative writing, music, film, and essays, almost all of them by Black artists and scholars. The curriculum is organized into thematic blocks, including 'Intersectionality', 'Memory and Memorialization', 'Resistance, Refusal, Fugitivity', and many others. Ward explains that the thematic organization is intended to be generative: it enables a transhistorical and translocational approach and gives students the freedom to make their own associations and comparisons between texts (Ward, 2021). The reading list is followed by prompts for writing and suggestions for reflective exercises. For instance, students are encouraged to set up their own reading groups, to design their own abolitionist curriculum, and to imagine a conversation between two different voices from the curriculum, to be written down in a form of their choosing.

'The abolitionist curriculum' originated as a response to the wide surge of interest in Black Lives activism after the police killings of Black Americans such as Breonna Taylor and George Floyd in 2020. As Ward (2021) puts it: 'I was getting really annoyed not only with the suggestion that issues such as antiBlack racism or state/police brutality were "new", but also that there were not significant historical legacies that lie behind these contemporary residues of antiBlackness.' As the only Black member of staff in a large English department, he wanted to actively move such conversations forward, both within and beyond the department. He chose the term 'abolitionist' to describe the curriculum because it immediately evokes the transatlantic slave trade, signalling the curriculum's emphasis on Blackness and anti-Black racism. In Ward's view, this term also carries a more radical potential and a stronger link to activism than the term 'decolonization' because of universities' appropriation of the language of decolonization to describe tokenistic diversity initiatives (see also Alessandrini, 2023; Jayawardane and

Walcott, 2021). He also wonders whether decolonizing the university is even possible: 'can an institution that directly created and promoted much of the theory of coloniality, and that is still a beneficiary of this, be divested of colonialism?!' He thus sees decolonization as cohering more easily with ideas of simply reforming the university, whereas abolition for him offers greater revolutionary possibilities (Ward, 2021).

In keeping with my argument in this book, Ward is concerned with addressing not just what, but how, we read. The key intervention of 'The abolitionist curriculum' in this regard is its attention to the contexts *in which* we read. By putting the student in charge of their own education, the curriculum encourages them to decide how they want to approach it. They have the freedom to decide what, when, and how much they read; whether to read individually or with others; and to actively consider what they themselves can add to the curriculum. Ward also notes that, while the curriculum centres and celebrates Blackness, it does not address only Black readers: it seeks to increase everyone's knowledge and to inspire and uplift each reader. His 'hope for the curriculum is that it inspires more conversation and critical thinking amongst its readers – this is what I think is the genesis for any concrete actions or change to take place. Resulting from this, I hope that the readers of this translate these conversations and thoughts into actions that effect or contribute to the abolition of antiBlackness' (Ward, 2021).

Ward's comments point to a belief shared by all efforts to decolonize literary studies in the sense in which I have been using the term in this book. The imperative to restructure our degree programmes, expand our sources of knowledge, and think from where we stand also indicates the responsibility to link our reading to wider struggles within and beyond our local communities and to actively contribute to those struggles. The rest of this book works through four different ways of approaching literary texts that help us to recognize the urgent political questions that they raise and foreground their relationships to past and present movements for equality and justice.

Reflection III: Decolonizing your curriculum

1. What changes would you make to the literature curriculum in your department or degree programme? How might the principles of decolonization (as you understand them) inform these changes?
2. Which of the changes that you envision would be easy to implement? Which might be more difficult? What kinds of obstacles or challenges do you foresee?
3. What do you think are the main barriers to changing the ways that literature students are taught to read? How can these barriers be addressed?
4. What strategies do you currently use to address the form and style of a text in relation to its political or historical location? What difficulties have you encountered in trying to develop such readings?

–3–

Language and Translation: What Is 'English' Literature?

This chapter introduces the first of four key ways to decolonize literary studies by engaging closely with the language of the texts we read, whether we read them in their original language or in translation. An obvious limitation of the wide-ranging approach to literary studies that I have been advocating is that it is not possible for one person to read everything. This means that an individual's reading must be selective, even as they seek to maintain an awareness of each text's relationship to a broader constellation of literary traditions and histories. The language in which a text is written presents one of the most challenging limits to the breadth of our reading. Evidently, we cannot hope to decolonize literary studies without challenging the global hegemony of English. This means fighting for more access to and support for language study for students in anglophone schools and universities, where the study of other languages has long been in decline. It also requires support for the study of languages other than English in non-anglophone contexts and more institutional recognition (in schools, libraries, cultural venues, government offices, etc.) of the multilingual nature of all societies.[8]

At the same time, however, even with enough opportunity and resource there is a limit to the number of languages that

Language and Translation 55

one person can become literate in. Thus, we also need more literary translation between a wider range of languages, as well as conscious strategies for reading texts in translation and in different versions of English and other hegemonic languages. As Emily Apter has observed, 'if translation failure is acceded to too readily, it becomes an all-purpose expedient for staying narrowly within one's own monolingual universe' (2006, p. 91).[9] When we read in translation, we need to remain aware of the imbalance of power between languages, which means that while some texts get translated others do not, and that far more texts are translated from English than into it. We must also bear in mind the many particularities of cultural and historical reference, written and oral tradition, and intellectual history that can be lost in translation. However, reading in translation – like reading in another language or in a regional version of a colonial language – can also highlight the fact that all reading involves interpretation and translation of some kind (historical, cultural, political), since all reading is 'about transitions from one realm, one area of human experience to another' (Said, 2004, p. 80). It also reminds us that, even if 'exact' translation from one language to another is impossible, languages are 'interrelated in what they want to express', as the German philosopher Walter Benjamin famously put it: the German and French words for bread (*Brot* and *pain*) are not interchangeable, and yet 'the two words mean the very same thing' (Benjamin, 2019 [1955], pp. 13, 17). The idea of *wanting* to express something is important here: Benjamin insists that the primary function of language is to communicate, and that translation facilitates and extends this essential purpose.

This chapter brings together several interventions on the question of language that have been influential in postcolonial and world literature studies in order to draw out their implications for the task of decolonizing literature as a discipline. I begin by summarizing some of the debates over literature written in English in the former British colonies after independence, which are also relevant to postcolonial francophone, Hispanophone, and lusophone contexts. One strand of these debates addressed the decision to write in English

56 Language and Translation

in contexts (primarily Africa and South Asia) where writers also had the option of writing in a pre-colonial language. Another addressed contexts in which writers generally did not have that option (notably the Caribbean, but also former settler colonies such as the United States, Canada, Australia, New Zealand, and Ireland), focusing on writers working in local versions of English. I revisit these debates via arguments made by Chinua Achebe (Nigeria); Ngũgĩ wa Thiong'o (Kenya); Salman Rushdie, Amit Chaudhuri, and S. Shankar (India), M. NourbeSe Philip (Tobago), and Kamau Brathwaite (Barbados). While Achebe (1997 [1965]) claimed English as a language of African literature, Ngũgĩ (1986) rejected this stance, declaring his 'farewell to English' in favour of his native Gĩkũyũ, as I also discussed in chapter 1. More recently, in response to the international publishing boom in anglophone Indian fiction, Rushdie (Rushdie and West, 1997) offered his own defence of Indian writing in English, while Chaudhuri (2001) challenged Rushdie's assertion of this literature's superiority. Meanwhile, in the Caribbean context, Philip (2015 [1989]) and Brathwaite (1993 [1979/81]) have claimed Caribbean English as a literary language in its own right, though their emphasis on the grounding of this language in African-Caribbean history and experience puts them closer to Ngũgĩ and Chaudhuri than to Achebe and Rushdie.

I then link these arguments to contemporary debates about the limitations and possibilities of reading in translation, which have become more prominent with the turn from postcolonial to world literature. While scholars such as Gayatri Chakravorty Spivak and Emily Apter challenge the 'monolinguist superiority' (Spivak, 2000, p. 410) of anglophone postcolonial and world literature studies, others caution against what the Warwick Research Collective calls the 'fetishism of language' (WReC, 2015, p. 27), by which they mean the privileging of professional linguistic expertise over other interpretive perspectives. The second group of critics tend to downplay what is lost in translation and instead commend what is gained, including the transmission of knowledge and the facilitation of connections between geographically dispersed struggles (Baker, 2016). Like the debates over the status of English in the former British colonies, the debates about reading in translation demand that we as readers consider where we stand in relation to language and that we recognize the fundamental inequality of languages in the current world order, while also working to challenge this inequality in our reading, learning, and teaching.

Reflection: The languages of postcolonial literature

1. For writers from former European colonies, what do you think that the advantages and disadvantages of writing in the colonial language might be? Why might a writer choose to write in the colonial language, and why might they decide to write in a pre-colonial language instead? In what circumstances might a writer have no choice but to write in a colonial language?
2. Do you think that colonial languages can adequately express the experiences of currently or formerly colonized people? Why or why not?
3. What are the drawbacks of reading only in English or other European languages from the perspective of decolonizing literary studies?
4. How can we as readers, students, and educators of literature challenge the dominance of English (and to a lesser extent, other European languages) in contemporary literary studies?
5. For readers whose formal education has been partly or entirely in English, to what extent have you been encouraged to study languages other than English as part of your literary and/or general education? What obstacles have you faced? If you speak a language other than English in which you haven't been formally educated (e.g. as a native or heritage speaker), to what extent have you been able to use it in your studies or in other institutional settings?

'A new English'?: Anglophone literature in Africa and South Asia

In postcolonial Africa and South Asia, most English-language writers have been multilingual, speaking at least one pre-colonial indigenous language as well as English. That means that these writers have made a deliberate choice to write in English, since it is not the only language available to them. This might be because English was the language of their education and is therefore what they feel most comfortable writing in. It might also be for reasons of audience: the global dominance of English means that writing in English can increase a writer's chances of reaching an international readership, as well as a national audience that isn't limited to their own linguistic group. The latter consideration is particularly relevant in extremely linguistically diverse countries such as India and Nigeria. Writers might also choose to use English because they want to 'write back' (Ashcroft et al., 2002) to the history of empire by making English language and literature reflect their own country or region's history.

In the essay 'English and the African writer' (1965), Achebe draws on each of these arguments to defend his own decision to write in English, with particular emphasis on its capacity to connect writers and readers across Nigeria and the African continent. Achebe doesn't see its colonial legacy as immutable; on the contrary, he argues that English can 'carry the weight of my African experience. But it will have to be a new English, still in full communion with its ancestral home, but altered to suit its new African surroundings' (Achebe, 1997, pp. 348–9). However, Achebe's optimistic take on English's expressive potential for African writers is complicated by questions of class and access. In much of Africa (like South Asia), literacy in English signals that the speaker has reached a certain level of education, which generally also means that they occupy a privileged economic and class position. This raises the question of *which* readers and writers can connect to one another through literature in

Language and Translation 59

English (though literature's universal status as an elite form means that this is true of literature in any language). Achebe's defence of English is further complicated by its post-imperial status as a language of global neocolonial domination, one that 'seeks everywhere to become the preeminent medium of cosmopolitan exchange' (Mufti, 2016, p. 146), including in places that were never subject to British rule. Can English simply be 'altered to suit' the self-expression and representation of people who have been victims, rather than agents, of this will to power?

In *Decolonising the Mind*, Ngũgĩ argues that it cannot. He is scathing about African writers whom he sees as having betrayed their native languages by writing in English, singling out Achebe's essay for special criticism:

> Why, we may ask, should an African writer, or any writer, become so obsessed by taking from his mother-tongue to enrich other tongues? Why should he see it as his particular mission? We never asked ourselves: how can we enrich our languages? How can we 'prey' on the rich humanist and democratic heritage in the struggles of other people in other times and places to enrich our own? (1986, p. 8)

Ngũgĩ makes it clear that he is unconvinced by Achebe's claim that African writers can make English reflect local experience. As I noted in chapter 1, Ngũgĩ sees language as a way of conveying the worldview of a culture, and thus as 'inseparable from ourselves as a community of human beings with a specific form and character, a specific history, a specific relationship to the world' (ibid., p. 16).

The use of 'ourselves' in this passage is distinct from that in Ngũgĩ, Owuor Anyumba, and Liyong's essay 'On the abolition of the English department', discussed in chapter 2. Here, Ngũgĩ is referring not to a national or continental 'we' but to a more restricted community defined by a shared language, specifically Ngũgĩ's first language Gĩkũyũ, which is spoken primarily in Kenya by a significant proportion (but not a majority) of the population. Ngũgĩ presents his

60   Language and Translation

decision to stop writing in English and write only in Gĩkũyũ
as an effort to 'restore the Kenyan child to his[10] environment
... With that harmony between himself, his language and
his environment as his starting point, he can learn other
languages and even enjoy the positive humanistic, democratic
and revolutionary elements in other people's literatures and
cultures without any complexes about his own language,
his own self, his own environment' (1986, pp. 28–9). In
other words, by helping to establish a written literature in
Gĩkũyũ – a language whose cultural production historically
had been primarily oral – Ngũgĩ seeks to undo the damaging
effects of a colonial and postcolonial education system that
presents English as the sole location of knowledge, power,
and value. Why bother to indigenize English as a language
of African literature, he argues, when African writers already
have languages at their disposal that carry the legacies of
the pre-colonial past and the struggle against colonialism
rather than the legacy of empire? Ngũgĩ is concerned less
with the question of whether this writing will be able to
reach speakers of other languages in Africa or the rest of
the world (although he is also a strong advocate of literary
translation, as I will discuss later in this chapter) than with
the need to create literature in the African languages that
are 'the collective memory bank of a people's experience in
history' (ibid., p. 15). He sees the development of literature
in pre-colonial African languages as a necessary foundation
for any wider engagement with other literatures and cultures,
as he and his colleagues also argue in the 'Abolition' essay.[11]

A related debate about English-language writers, their
audience, and the politics of their work has taken place
among South Asian writers, with particular fervour in post-
independence India and the Indian diaspora. One aspect
of the debate in this context is the idea that English can be
used as a neutral language that doesn't carry the same references to caste and religion that other Indian languages do.
For instance, speakers of Kashmiri, Hindi, Tamil, and other
pre-colonial languages might use English to avoid certain
markers of caste or religion or taboo subjects (Kachru,
2006 [1990], p. 273). This idea can arguably extend to

Language and Translation 61

the claim that Indian literature in English is more 'neutral' (meaning less closely associated with a particular ethnic or religious group) than literature written in pre-colonial Indian languages, though this claim is weakened by the strong association of English with economic and class privilege in the Indian subcontinent, as I have already noted. The claim of English's neutrality is further challenged by the phenomenal global success of anglophone Indian fiction in the last few decades. In the early years of this boom, Salman Rushdie, who remains the most widely internationally recognized Indian writer, controversially argued in the introduction to an anthology of post-independence Indian literature that Indian writing in English is 'stronger and more important' than that in other Indian languages, representing 'perhaps the most valuable contribution India has yet made to the world of books' (Rushdie and West, 1997, p. x). Rushdie thus went well beyond Achebe by proclaiming not only the pragmatic utility of English but also its artistic superiority. As Priyamvada Gopal observes, Rushdie's remarks 'served to inflame an already polarized situation', not least because he made no acknowledgement of the profoundly inequitable resources and reach of anglophone writing (2009, pp. 1–2).

The novelist and critic Amit Chaudhuri, in his introduction to his own subsequent anthology of Indian writing, caustically notes that to name contemporary anglophone Indian writers such as Amitav Ghosh, Arundhati Roy, and Rushdie himself as India's most important literary figures is like a reader of British literature being 'ignorant of the existence of Clare, Blake, Dickens and Lawrence' and believing that commercially successful contemporary novels by Julian Barnes or Martin Amis are 'the central texts of English literature, of English consciousness' (2001, p. xvii). By way of rebuttal, Chaudhuri's anthology consists mainly of texts in English translation from other Indian languages from the early nineteenth century onwards, though this approach still addresses anglophone readers and does not address the problem of the lack of translation between pre-colonial Indian languages. A decade later, the novelist and critic S. Shankar offered a similarly robust defence of literature in pre-colonial Indian languages, which he (like Rushdie) termed 'vernacular' languages. Shankar rejects Rushdie's dismissal of this writing as aesthetically simplistic and 'parochial' (2012, p. 4). For Shankar, far from being 'backward', literature in vernacular languages importantly emphasizes 'locality and particularity with regard to geographical region' and so challenges the tendency in much influential postcolonial writing and scholarship to privilege the transnational over the local (ibid., pp. 11, 19). Moreover, this kind of local sensibility is not limited to literature in pre-colonial languages but can also appear in English-language texts such as that of the novelist R. K. Narayan, who set his extensive body of work in the fictional South Indian town of Malgudi (ibid., p. 22).

Shankar's example of Narayan recalls Gopal's insistence that anglophone Indian writing is a 'heterogeneous and capacious body of work', meaning that sweeping condemnation is as inaccurate as indiscriminate praise (2009, p. 3). The same is true of anglophone African literature. In order to decolonize dominant approaches to literature from these contexts, then, we need to historicize and situate African and South Asian writing in English, while also working to improve the conditions for the study of pre-colonial indigenous languages and the production and circulation of literature written in and translated from those languages.

Summary

- In anglophone Africa and South Asia, anglophone writers often speak at least one African or South Asian language besides English. These writers may decide to work in English because (1) it is the language of their education, or (2) to reach a wider national or global audience, or (3) to claim English as a local language with the capacity to reflect local ways of thinking and perceiving (Achebe, 1997; Rushdie and West, 1997).

Language and Translation

- However, other writers, most famously Ngũgĩ wa Thiong'o (1986), have argued that English cannot be seen as a local language like any other because of its history as a language of colonial domination. Ngũgĩ argues that African writers have a social and political responsibility to write in pre-colonial indigenous languages, which he sees as carrying the worldviews and histories of particular language communities.
- The currency of anglophone African and South Asian fiction in the global literary marketplace presents additional complications, since this writing tends to be received as representative of 'African' or 'Indian' experience despite its emergence from a small, privileged class of writers (Gopal, 2009).
- One way of challenging this perception is to make more writing in pre-colonial South Asian and African languages available in English translation (e.g. Chaudhuri, 2001), though this does not address the need for translation between pre-colonial indigenous languages or the need for more language study and opportunities for publication of literature in these languages.

'I have no mother tongue': anglophone literature in the Caribbean

M. NourbeSe Philip's poem 'Discourse on the logic of language' (1989) begins: 'English is my mother tongue / A mother tongue is not / not a foreign lan lan lang / language / l/anguish / anguish / – a foreign anguish.' Though the poem opens with the apparently simple statement that English is the speaker's 'mother tongue' and thus their native language, the authority of this claim immediately breaks down. Philip associates the word 'language' with its near homonym 'languish', and then the rhyme 'anguish', replacing the sense of comfort and belonging that the phrase 'mother tongue' connotes with allusions to stasis and suffering. As the poem continues, the presumption that the speaker has a natural or easy relationship to English becomes impossible to sustain: 'English is / my father tongue. / A father tongue is / a foreign language ... I have no mother / tongue ... I must therefore be tongue / dumb / dumb-tongued / dub-tongued / damn dumb / tongue' (2015, p. 30). There is a tension here between the poet's use of wordplay and experiments with sound, which demonstrate a subversive mastery of the language, and the content of the poem, which expresses a profound alienation from English and a resulting sense of linguistic breakdown and wordlessness.

Philip thus draws the reader's attention to the complex status of English in the Caribbean. As in anglophone Africa and South Asia, English is the language of the history of colonial domination in the region, alongside French and Spanish. However, unlike in Africa and South Asia, in the Caribbean there is no pre-colonial language that is widely spoken today. This is because of the region's history of catastrophic colonial violence. Spanish colonizers first arrived in the region in the late fifteenth century and went on to kill most of the indigenous population of Taíno, Caribs, and other Indigenous American peoples through violence and disease. From the early seventeenth century, British and other European traders began to forcibly transport West African people to the region to work as slaves, until the slave trade was abolished in 1807. These populations were forbidden from speaking their many different native languages, making English the only permissible and common language. This was also true of the South Asian indentured labourers who came to the Caribbean after the abolition of the slave trade. The dominant language that is spoken on the anglophone islands today is a form of English inflected by the pronunciation and syntax of the languages that enslaved African people spoke: this is sometimes called patois/patwa, or creole, or simply Caribbean English. On other Caribbean islands, Spanish and French creoles are spoken. Thus, in the anglophone Caribbean, the question writers face is not whether to write in English, since there is no other widely

Language and Translation 65

shared language, but how to make English reflect local knowledge and experience.

In his essay 'History of the voice' (1993), Kamau Brathwaite influentially describes how Caribbean English speakers and writers have created a language that rises to this challenge through not only its vocabulary and subject matter but also its rhythms and syntax. The first half of the essay deals with the social and linguistic history of English in the Caribbean. Brathwaite argues that the plantation owners' suppression of African languages among enslaved people served an 'interesting intercultural purpose': the language that the enslaved people came to speak was transformed 'from a purely African form to a form that was African, but which was adapting to the new environment and to the cultural imperatives of the European languages' (1993, p. 262). He identifies the development of a whole new kind of English based on African syntax, pronunciation, and cadence and thus presents Caribbean English as a hybrid cultural practice: it combines elements of different languages to produce something new.

Brathwaite then goes on to set up a parallel between the historical suppression of African languages and the ongoing suppression of local knowledge and modes of expression in the Caribbean educational system, echoing Ngũgĩ's argument about colonial education in Kenya. He argues that, even after independence, the system continued to privilege colonial literature and culture:

> [T]he creole adaptation to all this is the child who, instead of writing in an essay 'the snow was falling on the playing fields of Shropshire' (which is what our children literally were writing until a few years ago, below drawings they made of white snow fields and the corn-haired people who inhabited such a landscape), wrote 'the snow was falling on the cane fields' ... She was trying to have both cultures at the same time. But that is creolization. (1993, pp. 263–4)

In place of this sense of alienation and incoherence, Brathwaite calls for Caribbean English speakers to recognize

66 Language and Translation

and celebrate the existence of what he calls 'nation language'. 'Nation language', he writes, 'is the language which is influenced very strongly by the African model, the African aspect of our New World/Caribbean heritage. English it may be in terms of its lexicon, but it is not English in terms of its syntax' (ibid., pp. 265–6). He goes on to list some of the characteristics of nation language. First, it is derived from an oral tradition, which means 'the noise that it makes is part of the meaning' (ibid., p. 271). (There is an explicit engagement with this idea in Philip's poem, which plays not just with the connotations but also the sound of different words for 'mother': 'my mammy tongue / my mummy tongue / my momsy tongue / my modder tongue / my ma tongue'.) Second, nation language is based on the rhythm of the calypso, rather than pentameter like the English poetic canon (ibid., p. 272). Finally, nation language is part of a 'total expression' of the community, unlike the 'isolated' and 'individualistic' experience of reading the texts of the English canon. This is because oral tradition depends on the interaction between the poet and the audience: 'the noise and sounds that the poet makes are responded to by the audience and are returned to him' (ibid., p. 273).

Thus, although Caribbean 'nation language' is not a pre-colonial indigenous language in the same way that (say) Gĩkũyũ or Tamil are, it also carries the history of resistance to slavery and colonialism in its sound and structure. A number of twentieth- and twenty-first-century anglophone Caribbean writers, especially poets, have chosen to use the syntax, vocabulary, and phonetic spelling of 'nation language' in their work in order to challenge the dominance of the English literary canon and inscribe Caribbean English as a language of literary expression. Celebrated examples include Brathwaite himself, the Jamaican poet Louise Bennett (popularly known as Miss Lou, whom Brathwaite discusses at some length in his essay), and the British-Jamaican poet Linton Kwesi Johnson, among many others.

Not all anglophone Caribbean poets choose to write in this way, however, and some poets choose to do it in some poems and not others. In this regard, the decision about what

Language and Translation 67

kind of English to write in can be seen as an artistic as well as a political choice, meaning that a writer who uses Caribbean English is not necessarily more 'authentic' than one who does not. As Philip puts it:

> To say that the experience [of Caribbean writers] can only be expressed in standard English (if there is any such thing) or only in the Caribbean demotic (there *is* such a thing) is, in fact, to limit the experience for the African artist working in the Caribbean demotic. It is in the *continuum of expression* from standard to Caribbean English that the veracity of the experience lies. (2015, p. 84)

Philip's claim is partly descriptive, in its identification of the 'continuum' of different registers and modes of speech that Caribbean English speakers encounter and use in their daily lives. However, it also invokes an encompassing understanding of the English language that includes and equally values all its speakers and variations. The challenge that anglophone Caribbean writers face, Philip continues, 'is to use the language in such a way that the historical realities are not erased or obliterated, so that English is revealed as the tainted tongue it truly is. Only in so doing will English be redeemed' (ibid., p. 85). Here, Philip echoes Achebe's assertion that the English language can convey the histories and experiences of more than one group of people, but she offers a fuller reckoning with the violence that has brought about this situation. She acknowledges the status of English as the shared language of the descendants of both enslaving and enslaved people and seeks to imagine where we might go from here.

Philip and Brathwaite remind us that a key part of the task of reading Caribbean writing in English, as well as any anglophone writing from formerly colonized regions, is to be aware of the status of the English language in the context that a given text comes from. This includes thinking about how a text responds to that context and being alert to its use of syntax, sound, rhythm, vocabulary, spelling, presentation, and register. Reading in this way might mean seeking out the writer's own statements on their use of language; finding out what other critics (especially critics from that regional and linguistic context) have said about it; and reading more widely across writing from that region, to be able to compare one writer's use of language with that of others. The English language cannot be cleansed of its imperial history or its contemporary will to dominance, but it is crucial to recognize that literature in English also includes an enormous body of writing that seeks to expose, resist, and overcome that legacy.

Summary

- In the anglophone Caribbean, English is both a language of colonial domination and the only common language. This means that anglophone Caribbean writers usually have no choice but to write in English and must grapple with the challenge of making the language reflect local histories and experience.
- The form of English that is spoken on the anglophone Caribbean islands today (like the forms of French and Spanish spoken on the other Caribbean islands) is shaped by the syntax and sound of the languages that were spoken by the West African people who were forcibly transported to the region as slaves. Kamau Brathwaite (1993) calls this form of English 'nation language', identifying it as an entirely new language that has developed in response to its environment.
- Brathwaite describes three key characteristics of 'nation language': it is derived from the oral tradition, so that its sound is part of its meaning; it is based on the rhythm of the calypso rather than pentameter; and it is part of the collective 'total expression' of the community rather than an individualistic mode of expression.

Language and Translation

- Many major anglophone Caribbean writers in the twentieth and twenty-first centuries, especially poets, have chosen to write in 'nation language'. However, Philip (2015) argues against conceiving a binary opposition between 'standard' and Caribbean English. Instead, she says, the language available to Caribbean English speakers should be understood as a continuum. Philip tasks Caribbean writers with the responsibility to use English in a way that recognizes its 'tainted' historical legacy.
- As readers seeking to decolonize our discipline, we are obliged to consider the status of English in the context from which a given text comes and to attend to the writer's use of language with that wider context in mind.

Reading in translation: limitations and possibilities

While much of the discussion of the status of language in postcolonial literary studies in the 1980s and 1990s focused on literature written in English, the subsequent turn to world literature has brought greater attention to literature written in other languages. As a result, a wide range of texts from postcolonial and other non-European contexts where English is not a major language of literary production are now regularly read in English translation by anglophone students and scholars. This includes texts by writers from francophone Africa and the Caribbean (e.g. Frantz Fanon, Aimé Césaire, Maryse Condé, Alain Mabanckou, Véronique Tadjo, Assia Djebar, Tahar Ben Jelloun), Hispanophone and lusophone Latin America (e.g. Gabriel García Márquez, Pablo Neruda, Octavio Paz, Isabelle Allende, Machado de Assis, Clarice Lispector, Jorge Luis Borges, Roberto Bolaño), the Arabophone Middle East and North Africa (e.g. Ghassan Kanafani, Mahmoud Darwish, Abdelrahman Munif, Tayeb Salih, Naguib Mahfouz, Nawal El-Saadawi, Elias Khoury,

70 Language and Translation

Sahar Khalifeh), and Sinophone China (e.g. Lu Xun, Mo Yan, Yan Lianke, Gao Xingjian, Yu Hua, Ma Jian, Can Xue).

As I outlined at the start of this chapter, this expansion of the purview of postcolonial and world literature studies has been accompanied by a renewed attention to the politics of translation. The participants in these debates nearly always acknowledge the imbalance of power between languages in the historical and contemporary world order, often with reference to Tejaswini Niranjana's (1992) important study of the colonial use of translation to perpetuate hierarchies of language and race (see e.g. Bassnett, 2013, p. 343). However, they differ in their recommendations about how students and scholars should respond. Prominent comparative literature scholars have warned against the decline of language study and the ability to read literature in the original language that their discipline has prized. They present this approach as a means of challenging the global dominance of English, though without always acknowledging that Euro–US formations of comparative literature have preserved the dominance of other European imperial languages. Other scholars have countered this view by championing the benefits of reading in translation, emphasizing translation's capacity to forge connections across linguistic, geographical, and other forms of distance and arguing that translation should be seen as a form of literary craft, creativity, and activism in its own right.

Gayatri Chakravorty Spivak, whom I discussed in the context of her standing in postcolonial literary studies in chapter 1, has also been one of the most prominent critics of the Anglocentrism of this field and the Eurocentrism of comparative literature in North America and Western Europe. In a famous intervention, she argues that literary and cultural studies should 'include the open-ended possibility of studying all literatures, *with linguistic rigor and historical savvy*' (2003, p. 13; emphasis added). The clause I have emphasized is important. Spivak wants to expand the remit of comparative literature to fully and equally include literature written in non-European languages, but she also wants to retain the 'old' comparative literature's emphasis on regional and historical expertise and 'the skill of reading closely in

Language and Translation 71

the original' language (ibid., p. 13). Her argument is based in part on her belief (like Ngũgĩ's) that ideas and experiences expressed in a language are specific to that language, and that translating them into English subsumes their particularity 'into the law of the strongest', as she argues elsewhere (2000, p. 400). She thus sees language study as an ethical imperative, especially for native English speakers: 'if you are interested in talking about the other, and/or in making a claim to be the other, it is crucial to learn other languages' (ibid., p. 407). This is not an argument against translation per se (Spivak herself is a prominent translator from French and Bengali into English) but, rather, a reproach to English-speaking scholars of any race or ethnicity who claim expertise in non-anglophone and especially non-European subject areas without knowing the languages of the people or places they study.

Emily Apter, a US scholar of comparative literature and French, goes further than Spivak in her assertion of the limits of translation as a form of knowledge. Although her first book on this subject took a more measured view, arguing that the 'challenge of Comp Lit is to balance the singularity of untranslatable alterity against the need to translate *quand même* [anyway]' (2006, p. 91), in *Against World Literature* (2013) she endorses the idea of 'untranslatability' more forthrightly. She explains this change in her position as a critical response to the rapid rise of world literature studies, which she sees as an 'entrepreneurial, bulimic drive to anthologize and curricularize the world's cultural resources' (ibid., p. 9). She resists the 'translatability assumption' that she says underpins this field by investigating examples of incommensurability, incomparability, mistranslation, and translation failure (ibid., pp. 9, 12). Her idea of 'untranslatability' thus refuses a pragmatic defence of translation that prioritizes the need to communicate, pointing instead to translation's inability to overcome what she presents as an absolute difference between languages.

An alternative to an emphasis on translation failure or inadequacy is to look more closely at how efforts to communicate across linguistic and cultural divides work in practice.

For instance, postcolonial critics have paid a great deal of attention to representations of contact between colonizers and colonized in European imperial languages (e.g. Pratt, 1993) but have had less to say about interactions between non-European languages and groups. Karima Laachir, Sara Marzagora, and Francesca Orsini's (2018) important work on 'multilingual locals and significant geographies' challenges this oversight by attending to encounters between languages and literatures in specific non-European multilingual sites – North India, the Horn of Africa, and the Maghreb (North Africa) – where both European and African or Asian languages are spoken. This allows them to emphasize 'south–south' comparisons and relationships and to insist that we conceive of 'the world' as 'always a view from somewhere', echoing but also resituating the invitation to think from where we stand that I discussed in chapter 2. Like Spivak and Apter, Laachir, Marzagora, and Orsini emphasize the importance of working in original languages, but they prioritize the interactions between languages rather than the barriers between them. Among areas that they suggest for investigation are multilingual networks of writers and thinkers; traces of other languages within monolingual texts; the interaction of written and oral forms; and diverse routes of literary circulation, including the circulation of texts in translation (ibid., p. 19). Relatedly, Rachael Gilmour reminds us of 'the *everydayness* of multilingual subjectivity' (2020, p. 1), even in countries as ideologically monolingualist as the United Kingdom and the United States, where many millions of people use more than one language. Gilmour argues that the work of contemporary British writers such as Vahni Capildeo, Suhayl Saadi, Daljit Nagra, Xiaolu Guo, and Brian Chikwava, who self-consciously incorporate multiple languages and linguistic registers into their writing, shows 'what happens when one stops translating a multilingual consciousness and experience of the world into monolingual English' (ibid.).

Each of these approaches requires that the literature student and scholar should be literate in, or at least conversant with, one or more languages besides English.

Language and Translation 73

However, other scholars have expressed concern about the risk of an uncritical celebration of language acquisition, since knowledge of a language does not automatically guarantee solidarity or reciprocity with the native speakers of that language. As I noted at the start of this chapter, the Warwick Research Collective criticizes the field of comparative literature for its tendency to 'hold up a merely *quantitative* notion of multilingual competence, to celebrate multilinguisticality as though it in itself conduced to social harmony and equality' (WReC, 2015, p. 25). While this gloss is not an entirely fair characterization of the arguments I have been summarizing, the collective are right to caution against the assumption of multilingualism's inherent good intentions. As they observe, many colonial administrators and Orientalist scholars were fluent in one or more of the languages of the regions they ruled (cf. Said, 1978); this continues to be the case in contemporary colonial and neo-imperial states such as the United States and Israel.[12] Expertise in a language is thus no guarantee of good-faith engagement with a particular language community or text. WReC also contend that we should be as concerned with what is gained in translation as what is lost. This means seeing both 'reading and translating as themselves social rather than solitary practices', involving a diverse collective of people including authors, publishers, readers, and translators (2015, p. 28; see also N. Harrison, 2015).

The Iranian-American cultural critic Hamid Dabashi (2013), in a reflection on his own education in Iran in the 1960s and 1970s, endorses this view. He recalls that the students and scholars of his generation 'read left, right, and center, then north and south ... with a voracious worldliness that had no patience for East or West of any colonial geography.' Dabashi makes no apology for their having read much of this work in translation and, like WReC, emphasizes the benefits: 'Works of philosophy – and their readers – gain in translation not just because their authors begin to breathe in a new language but because the text signals a world alien to its initial composition. Above all they gain because these authors and their texts have to face a new audience.' Dabashi focuses here on the encounter between text and reader, suggesting that the reader's effort to connect the ideas of a particular text to their own context and experience changes the text itself by demonstrating its relevance to a different situation than the one in which it was written. A text's ability to 'signal' to differently located audiences depends on multiple process of translation: not just linguistic, but also between histories, cultures, experiences, and beliefs. Indeed, Timothy Brennan argues that ideological or political translation can be an even more difficult translation than one between languages, and that it is often just as important for a reader to be able to identify a text's set of political references – particularly when that text positions itself as a contribution to a particular movement – as it is to recognize its historical, cultural, or linguistic references (2014, pp. 389–90).

Ngũgĩ offers a more pragmatic but equally ambitious defence of translation as a means of broadening access to the world's literatures and thus beginning to challenge the linguistic and economic hierarchies that privilege the circulation of some texts over others. In an interview, he describes translation as 'the common language of languages', explaining,

> I am not against English or any other language. What I totally oppose is the unequal relationship of power between them. English is not more of a language than any other language. ... I would like to see European, Asian, and Latin American literatures translated into African languages and vice versa. ... Own your language, add other languages to it: that is empowerment. (Dyssou, 2017)

Ngũgĩ refers approvingly in this interview to the project by the Nairobi-based Jalada writers' collective of translating one of his stories in Gĩkũyũ into 100 languages (at the time of writing), many of them African languages (Kilolo, 2016). A collective project of translation such as this may not overturn the profound imbalance of power between languages, but it offers a 'prefigurative' glimpse, as Mona Baker (2016) puts it, of what a horizontal and egalitarian landscape of translation might look like. Baker is referring, however, not to literary translation but to the use of translation in social movements, where the ability to translate the movement's vision, aims, and achievements into other languages is essential, since translation is 'precisely what enables protest movements to connect and share experiences across the globe.' She argues for a recognition of translators as 'full participants within non-hierarchical, solidarity activist communities' and for an understanding of translation within social movements as a prefigurative activity, meaning that it makes 'use of verbal, visual and aesthetic languages to construct an alternative world in the here and now' (ibid.; see also Antena Aire, 2020).

Baker reminds us that the circulation of ideas through literary translation has real consequences for movement organizing and collective resistance. Ideas make their way from one place to another through literature, film, journalism, visual art, social media platforms, and other cultural forms. They change along the way with each new community of interpreters, forging connections between the people who encounter and engage with them. Edward Said, in the essay I cited at the beginning of this chapter, offers the Islamic concept of *ijtihad* as a way of conceiving a community of readers engaged in a collective endeavour of interpretation, with each individual reader drawing on the efforts of those who have gone before them (2004, p. 68). While we cannot simply ignore the fact that a text that comes to us in translation, or in an English that differs from the version that we ourselves might speak, I would argue with Said, Dabashi, and the other thinkers I have been discussing that, rather than seeing our own response to that text as either authoritative or proscribed, we should instead be both aware of and curious about the route that a particular text has taken to reach us, and alive to the differences as well as the commonalities between the circumstances in which that text was written and our own. This is a form of situated reading that attends to 'the words and the structures in the books we read' but also extends our readings 'out into the various worlds each one of us resides in' (ibid., p. 76). This kind of reading might involve engaging with the language of a text in translation, a postcolonial form of an imperial language, a language that is not our own first language, or multiple languages, but it always requires humility, open-mindedness, and a willingness to question what we think we know.

Summary

- The world literature turn has led to an increased engagement in the anglophone academy with texts in translation from other languages, including non-European languages. This shift has produced a renewed interest in the politics of translation.
- Some critics (Spivak, 2000, 2003; Apter, 2013) have expressed concern about the implications of a wider reliance on translation, emphasizing the limits of what can be translated and the problematic politics of reading only in English.
- Another criticism of the world literature turn is that it assumes an imperial model of centre–periphery contact between European and non-European cultures instead of attending to the interactions between languages in specific multilingual locations in the Global South (Laachir et al., 2018).
- Other critics, however, have defended the practice of reading in translation. These critics challenge the idea that linguistic competence necessarily leads to more equal social relations (WReC, 2015) and emphasize the benefits of making texts as widely available as possible (Dabashi, 2013; Ngũgĩ in Dyssou, 2017). They also note that translation is not limited to language but also includes political, historical, and other kinds of translation (Brennan, 2014), and that translation is a crucial part of the spread of social movements (Baker, 2016).

Language and Translation

- A practice of situated reading – meaning that we are alert to a text's original context (linguistic and otherwise) but also consider its relationship to our own situation – can help us to position ourselves as part of a wider community of readers engaged in a collective endeavour of interpretation and enquiry.

–4–
'A Comparative Literature of Imperialism': Reading Colonial and Anticolonial Texts Together

This chapter introduces a second way of decolonizing literary studies, focusing on how we understand the relationship between texts written from colonial and anticolonial points of view. It revisits two established approaches to this question: (1) the idea of 'writing back', in which texts from formerly colonized countries are read as a repudiation of European imperialism and thus as a form of anticolonial activism (Marx, 2004, pp. 85–6); and (2) the idea of 'contrapuntal' reading, which holds that colonial and anticolonial texts must be read together in order to conceive the histories of imperial domination and anti-imperialist resistance as an interconnected whole. Both concepts insist that colonial and anticolonial texts cannot be studied in isolation from one another. The idea of writing back does this in part by attending to texts that explicitly present themselves as adversarial rewritings of 'classic' works of European literature. Such rewritings have often emerged from a specific phase of anticolonial resistance that takes place either before or immediately after formal political independence. By contrast, contrapuntal reading is a more versatile method that can be applied to any pairing of texts with different standpoints in relation to the history of empire, in keeping with the inclusive and wide-ranging approach to literary

'A Comparative Literature of Imperialism' 79

analysis that characterizes the discipline of comparative literature. The idea of writing back is most closely associated with Bill Ashcroft, Gareth Griffiths, and Helen Tiffin's book *The Empire Writes Back* (1989), an early and influential work of postcolonial literary criticism. The book takes its title from an essay by the Indian novelist Salman Rushdie called 'The empire writes back with a vengeance' (1982). In this essay, Rushdie playfully appropriates the title of the second film in the Stars Wars franchise, *The Empire Strikes Back* (1980), to celebrate postcolonial writers' resistance to the political and cultural legacies of European imperialism ('empire' refers here to the people subjugated by colonial rule). Ashcroft, Griffiths, and Tiffin adapt this idea into a definition of postcolonial writing, which they see as 'the process by which the [colonial] language, with its power, and the writing, with its signification of authority, has been wrested from the dominant European culture' (2002, p. 7). To support their argument, they draw on the work of figures such as Ngũgĩ wa Thiong'o, Chinua Achebe, and Edward Said, along with a range of other anglophone anti- and postcolonial thinkers.

In the anglophone university literature curriculum, however, the idea of writing back typically refers more specifically to anti- and postcolonial writers' appropriations of canonical texts. This phenomenon has been considered to be so significant that introductory postcolonial literature modules are sometimes organized around pairings of canonical works of English literature and texts that respond directly to them, such as Daniel Defoe's *Robinson Crusoe* (1719) and J. M. Coetzee's *Foe* (1986), Charlotte Brontë's *Jane Eyre* (1847) and Jean Rhys's *Wide Sargasso Sea* (1966), Joseph Conrad's *Heart of Darkness* (1899) and Chinua Achebe's *Things Fall Apart* (1958), and William Shakespeare's *The Tempest* (1610/11) and Aimé Césaire's *Une tempête* (*A Tempest*, 1969), each of which is discussed in this chapter. This approach can be a very effective way of encouraging students to question their existing knowledge and assumptions, since it returns to texts that they may have

80   'A Comparative Literature of Imperialism'

encountered previously and makes these texts' connection to the history of British imperialism impossible to ignore. The anticolonial rewritings emphasize the colonial contexts of the earlier texts, refuse their naturalization of European political and cultural dominance, and offer a more accurate retelling of this history that foregrounds the perspectives of the colonized.

Contrapuntal reading also seeks to expose the falsehoods and omissions of imperial cultural production, but it opens the field of comparison to the entire body of modern colonial and anticolonial writing, which means that it is effectively a way of conceiving world literature. This use of the term 'contrapuntal' comes from Edward Said's book *Culture and Imperialism* (1993), his second major contribution to postcolonial literary studies after *Orientalism* (discussed in chapter 1). Said takes the term from music criticism, where it describes a piece of music that contains multiple melodies that sometimes compete with and sometimes complement one another but are all equally important. Transposed to literature, the term indicates the need to read any work written by a beneficiary of imperialism in relation to works written by imperialism's victims and opponents. Said describes this method as a 'comparative literature of imperialism' that allows the reader to consider 'the different experiences contrapuntally, as a set of what I call intertwined and overlapping histories' (1994 [1993], p. 18).

While Said's approach can be accused of being overly conciliatory or forgiving of imperialism, as Benita Parry (2010, pp. 455–7) has argued, his invitation to read as widely and comparatively as possible emphasizes the need to 'take account of both processes, that of imperialism and of resistance to it, which can be done by extending our reading of the texts to include what was once forcibly excluded' (Said, 1994, pp. 66–7). Said's formulation may no longer sound novel, since literary studies has already moved towards greater diversity and inclusivity in the last few decades, as I discussed in chapters 1 and 2. However, the call to read contrapuntally remains important because it privileges a history of political struggle that is obscured by

'A Comparative Literature of Imperialism' 81

the decontextualized notion of diversity, as I have argued in previous chapters. It reminds us that colonial and anticolonial texts have an antagonistic relationship to one another and frames 'the historical experience of imperialism' as a field of battle 'requiring intellectual and political choices' (ibid., p. 259). It therefore encourages readers to situate each text we read in its historical and ideological contexts, foregrounding the relations of domination and resistance it narrates and the political judgements it demands or conceals.

This chapter offers an overview of writing back and contrapuntal reading as interpretive methods and, ultimately, argues for the indispensability of comparative criticism for decolonizing literary studies. I first discuss some of the key examples of anticolonial appropriations of canonical colonial texts, focusing on Coetzee, Rhys, Achebe, and Césaire's distinct approaches to this task. I then offer an example of how to read colonial and anticolonial texts that are not so obviously connected alongside one another, by looking at texts by the French settler writer Albert Camus and the Arab-Amazigh writer Assia Djebar as contending representations of what Said calls 'the same Algeria' (1994, p. 259). This discussion contrasts Camus' ambivalent representations of his settler characters' colonial sensibilities with Djebar's explicit critiques of colonial – and postcolonial – coercion and violence, particularly against Algerian women. It seeks to demonstrate Said's insistence that reading and writing 'are never neutral activities' (ibid., p. 318) but, rather, an opportunity to challenge our received ideas and invigorate our political commitments.

> ### Reflection: Strategies for comparative reading
>
> 1. How have 'classic' works of English or other European or North American literature been introduced in your literary education to date? Have you been encouraged to read the work of writers such as Shakespeare, Dickens, or Austen in relation to the

history of empire? If so, how has this relationship been presented? If not, how have you been encouraged to approach them instead?

2. Have you been invited to read works from imperial and anti-imperial perspectives comparatively, and/or have you chosen to do so yourself? If so, what are some of the points of comparison and contrast that you've noticed between these works?

3. How do you think you might approach a text that explicitly presents itself as a rewriting of a canonical European text? What features or techniques would you expect to see in the text that 'writes back'?

4. Imagine that you are presented with a pair of texts written from two very different locations and perspectives, such as a nineteenth-century Australian settler poem and a sixteenth-century Nahuatl testimony of the Spanish conquest of what is now Mexico. What kinds of connections might you look for between these two texts? How might their relationship to the history of empire be brought to bear on your readings?

Writing back, writing forward

Within the category of explicit reworkings of key texts of European imperial dominance, a broad distinction can be made between (1) texts that primarily draw attention to the canon's silence about imperial violence; and (2) texts that point out the canon's omissions but also offer a truer history and invite the reader to imagine a more emancipatory future. J. M. Coetzee's *Foe* and Jean Rhys's *Wide Sargasso Sea* are examples of the first type of response; Chinua Achebe's *Things Fall Apart* and Aimé Césaire's *Une tempête* are examples of the second.

Foe and *Wide Sargasso Sea* are both written by descendants of white settlers – from the settler-colonial contexts of South

'A Comparative Literature of Imperialism' 83

Africa and the Caribbean island of Dominica, respectively – and were published shortly before the formal end of colonial rule in each country. Both novels have subsequently become classics of anglophone modernist/postmodernist literature in their own right. This status derives in part from their explicit allusiveness and intertextuality, through which they present themselves as 'already canonized', as Derek Attridge writes of *Foe* (2004, p. 68). However, the novels' significance also comes from their critical interrogation of the premises of the original texts. *Foe* retells Daniel Defoe's *Robinson Crusoe*, a classic tale of colonial conquest and capitalist individualism, from the point of view of an English woman called Susan Barton. Susan is shipwrecked with a man called Cruso and subsequently seeks to publish a novel about her experience with the help of the English writer Foe (the real Daniel Defoe's birth surname). She also tries – and fails – to give voice to Friday, Cruso's servant, who is an Indigenous Carib in Defoe's novel but a Black African in Coetzee's. The novel makes extensive use of eighteenth-century English vocabulary and syntax, a stylistic choice that foregrounds the novel's central 'question of those voices and stories that must be left out' of colonial historical accounts (Zimbler, 2014, p. 164) – including those of colonial women – by making the narrative resemble a newly discovered archival document.

Many of the critical responses to *Foe* have focused on Susan's failed attempts to communicate with Friday. In a scene near the end of the novel, when Susan tries to teach Friday to read and write in English, he fills his slate with 'eyes, open eyes, each set upon a human foot: row upon row of eyes upon feet: walking eyes' (Coetzee, 1987 [1986], p. 147). He then wipes the slate clean before she can show it to Foe. Gayatri Spivak reads this scene as an overt rewriting of the ending of Defoe's novel, in which Friday 'learns his master's speech ..., believes the culture of the master is better, and kills his other self to enter the shady plains of north-western Europe' (1990, p. 14). Coetzee's Friday, by contrast, refuses the 'master's speech': his inscriptions instead signal either a pre-colonial heritage that Susan and Foe do not

84   'A Comparative Literature of Imperialism'

know or his own original artwork. The novel's cryptic final scene connects the inaccessibility of Friday's point of view to his violent subjugation under imperial rule. An unidentified narrator finds the bodies of Susan, Foe, and Friday in Foe's house in present-day London. Susan and Foe's bodies are motionless, but Friday still has a pulse. The narrator hears 'the sounds of the island' issuing from his mouth and notices 'a scar like a necklace, left by a rope or chain' on his neck (Coetzee, 1987, pp. 154–5). The narrator then moves to the site of Susan's shipwreck and again finds Friday, who again is still alive. The narrator asks Friday what the ship is, but, instead of speaking, Friday opens his mouth and releases a stream that 'runs northward and southward to the ends of the earth' (ibid., p. 157). Coetzee's invocation of the horror genre evokes the immense horrors of slavery, murder, rape, theft, and civilizational and environmental destruction committed in the name of empire. The scene makes the point, as Jarad Zimbler puts it, that 'teaching Friday to read and write could never be sufficient; instead, one would need to discover a means of speaking with the dead' (2014, p. 167), meaning the many millions of people who did not survive imperial violence.

Rhys's *Wide Sargasso Sea* also invokes the devastating history of slavery, with particular attention to the diffusion of imperial violence within colonial societies. It retells Charlotte Brontë's *Jane Eyre*, which is often read as an early feminist novel, from the perspective of Bertha Mason, Rochester's 'mad' wife whom he keeps locked in the attic. Rhys amplifies Brontë's brief backstory for this character, who is described as a wealthy heiress from Jamaica that Rochester was tricked into marrying, leaving him unable to marry Jane Eyre. In Rhys's retelling, Bertha's real name is Antoinette, and like Rhys herself she comes from a former enslaver family whose fortunes have deteriorated after the abolition of slavery in 1833. Her 'mad' behaviour is the result of her abusive treatment by her family and Rochester, but, as Spivak puts it in her influential reading of the novel, it also 'suggests that so intimate a thing as personal and human identity might be determined by the politics of imperialism' (1985,

p. 250). Antoinette's misery cannot be separated from her location as a 'white cockroach' (Rhys, 1997 [1966], p. 64), a derogatory name for the white descendants of slaveholders. *Wide Sargasso Sea* thus exposes the limits of the feminist imaginary of *Jane Eyre*, which extends only to white English women within a bounded range of class positions, while also demonstrating the earlier novel's dependence on the political economy of the British empire.

The imperial violence to which *Foe* alludes is addressed more graphically in *Wide Sargasso Sea*. The novel opens with Antoinette's account of the burning of her family's estate, which kills her younger brother: 'his head hung back over her [mother's] arm as if he had no life at all and his eyes were rolled up so that you only saw the whites' (Rhys, 1997, p. 20). Among the jeering crowd outside the burning building, Antoinette sees a Black child, Tia, who has been her playmate. When Antoinette runs towards her, Tia throws a stone that cuts Antoinette's forehead and then begins to cry. Antoinette narrates: 'We stared at each other, blood on my face, tears on hers. It was as if I saw myself. Like in a looking-glass' (ibid., p. 24). Both the burning of the estate and Tia's throwing of the stone are acts of retaliatory violence, as described by Frantz Fanon: 'The violence which has ruled over the ordering of the colonial world ... will be claimed and taken over by the native at the moment when, deciding to embody history in his person, he surges into the forbidden quarters' (1963, p. 40). While Antoinette and Tia's friendship hints at the potential for a 'mutual and creative "interculturation" between white and black Creoles' in the postcolonial Caribbean (Mardorossian, 1999, p. 1077), the force of colonial violence and anticolonial counter-violence destroys this possibility. At the end of the novel, when Antoinette decides to set fire to Rochester's house and jump to her death (the event in Brontë's novel that finally allows Jane to marry Rochester), she connects this act of self-destruction directly to the burning of her family's estate and her violent separation from Tia: 'Tia was there. She beckoned to me and when I hesitated, she laughed. I heard her say, You frightened?' (Rhys, 1997, p. 123).

86   'A Comparative Literature of Imperialism'

This is not to say that Antoinette is represented primarily as a victim, or as more victimized than the novel's Black characters. Her own racist statements – such as the pronouncement that the faces of the people surrounding the burning estate all look the same (Rhys, 1997, p. 22) – are challenged by Rhys's inclusion of the voices of Black characters, most notably Christophine, who was formerly enslaved by Antoinette's family and continues to work for them after emancipation. Christophine is an 'articulate antagonist of patriarchal, settler and imperialist law' (Parry, 1987, p. 38): she rejects the post-emancipation pretence that the exploitation of Black people has ended, practises obeah healing in defiance of colonial prohibitions, and castigates Rochester for his treatment of Antoinette: 'You think you fool me? You want her money but you don't want her ... you wicked like Satan self!' (Rhys, 1997, p. 104). Christophine is admittedly a minor character rather than a protagonist, but her speech marks a 'space in which the colonized can be written back into history' (Parry, 1987, p. 39) in all their resistance, knowledge, and fortitude. Through Christophine, Rhys registers the presence of this untold history in her narrative rather than attempting to relay it herself.

As these summaries indicate, Coetzee's and Rhys's rewritings of canonical texts draw attention to the absence of the narratives of enslaved and colonized people from the colonial record, but they stop short of filling in the gaps. This task has been taken up robustly, however, by Black and other writers from formerly colonized countries, who have often situated it as part of a collective artistic endeavour that is expressly linked to anticolonial political movements. Commonly rewritten texts such as William Shakespeare's *The Tempest* and Joseph Conrad's *Heart of Darkness* can be seen a 'medium of exchange among writers and critics' across the formerly colonized world, forming 'a network that may have been enabled by European imperialism but that no empire ever fully managed' (Marx, 2004, pp. 90–1). This project might seem self-defeating, since it arguably preserves the canonical status of the source text by continuing to use it as a point of reference. However, it can also be seen as a necessary

'A Comparative Literature of Imperialism' 87

stage of cultural decolonization that emphasizes the rejection of colonial culture by openly contesting its values (Nixon, 1987, pp. 558, 569).

Conrad's *Heart of Darkness* has been a key site of cultural struggle because it tells the story of the English protagonist Marlow, who journeys up the Congo River into the 'darkness' of an undifferentiated 'Africa'. Anticolonial rewritings of this text challenge Conrad's depiction of Africa as inscrutable and unknowable – as the title of his novel implies – and thus merely as a 'setting and backdrop which eliminates the African as human factor' (Achebe, 1978, p. 9). Explicit retellings of *Heart of Darkness* include the Guyanese novelist Wilson Harris's *Palace of the Peacock* (1960) and the Sudanese novelist Tayeb Salih's *Mawsim al-hijra ila al-shamal* (*Season of Migration to the North*, 1969 [1966]), which both restage Marlow's journey upriver. Harris relocates this voyage to the Guyanese rainforest and refashions it as a quest for an anticolonial and anti-capitalist national identity rooted in a sense of responsibility to the land, with extensive reference to Indigenous Nahuatl, Mayan, Carib, and Arawak cosmologies (Fehskens, 2018; Niblett, 2013). *Mawsim al-hijra ila al-shamal* reverses Marlow's journey through its account of the protagonist Mustafa Sa'eed and his violent and self-destructive *hijra* (an Arabic word for migration that recalls the Prophet Muhammad's journey from Mecca to Medina) from the colonial periphery of rural Sudan to the imperial metropole of London. While this journey into the heart of imperial darkness consumes Mustafa Sa'eed and leaves him unable to resume a life in his native village, the novel also gestures towards the prospect of a better future after empire. In the final scene the narrator, floundering in the Nile River 'halfway between north and south' and beginning to drown, suddenly experiences a powerful desire to live and screams 'with all [his] remaining strength: "Help! Help!"' (Salih, 1991 [1966], pp. 168–9).

By contrast, Chinua Achebe's *Things Fall Apart* (the title is taken from the 1919 poem 'The second coming' by the Irish poet W. B. Yeats) does not write back to *Heart of Darkness* so overtly, although Achebe does directly accuse Conrad of

88   'A Comparative Literature of Imperialism'

racism in a much later essay on the novel (Achebe, 1978). Instead, it counters Conrad's portrayal of 'Africa', which can be seen as characteristic of the colonial representations of Africa that Achebe criticizes elsewhere (e.g. Achebe, 1975), by narrating daily life in an Igbo village before the arrival of the British colonizers. The villagers' way of life gradually disintegrates in the face of the Christian conversion of some of the members of the community and the imposition of British law and governance. One of the elders of the village, Obierika, observes: 'The white man is very clever. He came quietly and peaceably with his religion. We were amused at his foolishness and allowed him to stay. Now he has won our brothers, and our clan can no longer act as one. He has put a knife on the things that held us together and we have fallen apart' (Achebe, 2001 [1958]). This passage 'writes back' by retelling the story of the colonization of what is now Nigeria from the perspective of its victims. Instead of the 'pacification' of 'primitive tribes', as his character the District Commissioner puts it, Achebe tells the story of the wanton destruction of a complex society. The novel builds up a detailed portrait of a community that has its own methods of social organization, economic and political structures, religious practices, and artistic traditions. Achebe does not depict Igbo society as timeless or perfect: indeed, the Christian missionaries are successful primarily among marginalized members of the community, which suggests that inequalities within Igbo society helped to facilitate its conquest. However, the novel unequivocally refutes the view that Igbo people could in any way be described as 'primitive', or that they deserved to be colonized.

A comparable effort to draw on the cultural legacy of colonialism in order to supersede it can be seen in the many reworkings of Shakespeare's play *The Tempest*. Shakespeare has been a popular point of departure for anticolonial writers because of the colonial education system's use of his work to assert the supposed superiority of English culture. *The Tempest* became a particular target after the French social scientist Octave Mannoni (1950) used it to argue that colonized subjects (represented by Caliban) had become

'A Comparative Literature of Imperialism' 89

psychologically 'dependent' on their colonizers (represented by Prospero). Caribbean and African anticolonial intellectuals – among them Frantz Fanon, George Lamming, Roberto Fernández Retamar, Kamau Brathwaite, John Pepper Clark, Ngũgĩ wa Thiong'o, and David Wallace – emphatically rejected this idea and sought to reclaim Caliban as a heroic figure who valiantly expels Prospero from the island (Nixon, 1987, pp. 560–4, 573).

Aimé Césaire's play *Une tempête* (*A Tempest*) stands out for its emphasis on the irresolvable conflict between Caliban and Prospero (Nixon, 1987, p. 571). In this rewriting, Caliban's resistance takes the form of a reclamation of indigenous cultural forms and the creation of new ones, as well a refusal to compromise with the colonial power to secure his freedom. This stance is apparent from Caliban's first entrance onstage:

> CALIBAN: Uhuru!
> PROSPERO: What did you say?
> CALIBAN: I said, Uhuru!
> PROSPERO: Mumbling your native language again! I've already told you, I don't like it. (Césaire, 2002 [1969], p. 17)

This introduction contrasts with Caliban's first appearance in *The Tempest*, in which he enters cursing Prospero and his servant Ariel in English (Shakespeare, n.d. [1610/11], I.2.385). Césaire's Caliban introduces himself with a declaration of freedom in Swahili – 'Uhuru!' – using a word that gained currency within and beyond Africa during the mid-twentieth-century decolonization struggles (see also Nixon, 1987, p. 573). This is a crucial departure from the original text, for it emphasizes Caliban's pre-colonial African heritage as well as his participation in an international anticolonial liberation struggle. It is worth noting that Césaire explicitly names his intended actors and perhaps also his audience as Black: his play's original subtitle is '*Adaptation pour un théâtre nègre*' (adaptation for a Black theatre) (Césaire, 1969).

90 'A Comparative Literature of Imperialism'

However, Césaire also allusively mobilizes Shakespeare's wording to draw out the resistant potential of Caliban's character in the original play. Much of what Caliban says in the rest of this scene is taken directly from *The Tempest*. Shakespeare's Caliban asserts, 'This island's mine by Sycorax, my mother / Which thou tak'st from me' (I.2.395–6) and retorts to Prospero's claim to have given him language that 'my profit on 't / Is I know how to curse' (1.2.437–8). In Césaire's rewriting, Caliban similarly claims to be the 'King of the Island given to me by my mother Sycorax' and tells Prospero that 'You didn't teach me a thing! Except to jabber in your language so that I could understand your orders' (2002, p. 17). With these borrowings, Césaire underlines the imperial context of the original play, which was first written and performed in the early phase of European conquest. He highlights Shakespeare's own ambivalence about the imperial project and makes it impossible for anyone in the audience to return to Shakespeare's play without considering its relationship to empire.

The final scenes of *Une tempête* decisively position Caliban, not Prospero, as the play's 'preeminent historical agent' (Nixon, 1987, p. 571). In contrast to the original text, in which Prospero defeats Caliban's attempted rebellion and magnanimously allows him to continue in his service, Césaire's version foregrounds Caliban's ongoing resistance in a closing monologue:

> For years I bowed my head
> for years I took it, all of it ...
> But now, it's over!
> Over, do you hear? ...
> I'll impale you! And on a stake that you've
>   sharpened yourself!
> You'll have impaled yourself! ...
> And I know that one day
> my bare fist, just that,
> will be enough to crush your world!
> The old world is crumbling down! (Césaire, 2002,
>   pp. 61–2)

'A Comparative Literature of Imperialism' 91

This speech is very far from Caliban's final words in *The Tempest*, where he contritely promises to 'be wise hereafter / And seek for grace' (V.1.351–2). Césaire's Caliban vows to continue the struggle until victory, sustained by the justice of his cause and his belief that history is on his side. The audience are left with the spectacle of an 'aged and weary' Prospero staggering across the stage, shouting about opossums taking over the island: 'all this unclean nature! ... It's as though the jungle were laying siege to the cave'. From offstage, Caliban claims his triumph: 'FREEDOM HI-DAY! FREEDOM HI-DAY!' (Césaire, 2002, pp. 65–6). With this conclusion, Césaire forcefully rejects *The Tempest*'s closing affirmation of imperial rule as the natural order. In its place, he envisions a near future in which the colonial power has been defeated and the island's pre-colonial ecology has begun to recover. He invites his audience to go beyond the stage of rejecting the empire's authority to begin to imagine what kind of world we might build in its place.

Summary

- 'Writing back' can be used to describe any anti- or postcolonial writing that challenges imperial rule. However, the term is often more specifically used to refer to texts that overtly rewrite canonical European texts.
- These adversarial retellings of canonical texts can be divided into two categories: (1) texts that highlight the canon's silence about imperial violence; and (2) texts that draw attention to this silence while also narrating a truer history and inviting the reader to imagine a different future.
- Coetzee's rewriting of *Robinson Crusoe* in *Foe* and Rhys's rewriting of *Jane Eyre* in *Wide Sargasso Sea* both foreground the source texts' occlusion of the perspective of the colonized and enslaved. While the

rewritings mark a space where this story could be told, both novels refrain from telling it.

- By contrast, Black and other writers from formerly colonized countries have offered alternative histories of empire in their reworkings of canonical English texts. Conrad's *Heart of Darkness* and Shakespeare's *The Tempest* have been especially popular targets.
- Responses to *Heart of Darkness* by Harris, Salih, and Achebe challenge the use of 'Africa' as a backdrop for European endeavour. Their works narrate journeys by African and Caribbean protagonists and offer detailed accounts of pre-colonial indigenous knowledges, environments, and social systems.
- Among the many rewritings of *The Tempest*, Césaire's *Une tempête* is notable for its emphasis on the irreconcilable conflict between Prospero and Caliban, its celebration of Caliban's resistance, and its invocation of an emancipatory future.

Contrapuntal reading

A key means of distinguishing writing back from contrapuntal reading can be seen in the terms themselves. Writing back is a kind of *writing*: this concept emphasizes the author's conscious effort to challenge imperial domination and its legacies in the form and content of their work. Contrapuntal reading, on the other hand, is a strategy for *reading*, based on the premise that texts with different relationships to European empire can and should be read together so that the reader can better comprehend the interdependence of the histories of imperial domination and anti-imperial resistance. This method draws on comparative literature's disciplinary imperative 'to get a perspective beyond one's own nation, to see some sort of whole instead of the defensive little patch offered by one's own culture, literature, and history', as Said puts it (1994, p. 43). This stance echoes my argument in

'A Comparative Literature of Imperialism'   93

previous chapters that the decolonization of literary studies requires us to read as widely as we can, particularly in literatures that have been excluded or marginalized within our educational and cultural institutions. For people from metropolitan countries and/or based in metropolitan universities, it also recalls Priyamvada Gopal's suggestion that, if for Ngũgĩ in *Decolonising the Mind*, 'cultural decolonisation begins at home (first in Kenya, going on to wider Africa) ... perhaps "Europe's" engagement with decolonisation must begin in the other direction, i.e. with the world, as it undertakes an unflinchingly truthful engagement with the pivotal role of empire and colonialism in its own making' (2021, p. 879).

To offer a concrete example of what a contrapuntal approach might look like, the final section of this chapter considers a short story by Albert Camus, 'La femme adultère' (The adulterous woman', 1957), alongside Assia Djebar's story and essay collection *Femmes d'Alger dans leur appartement* (*Women of Algiers in their Apartment*, 1980). This is not an arbitrary pairing: both writers grew up in French colonial Algeria, but Camus was a member of the white French settler class, while Djebar (born Fatima-Zohra Imalayen) was a colonial subject until Algeria achieved formal independence in 1962. French rule in Algeria (like that of other European colonial regimes, including Britain's) depended on what Jill Jarvis calls a 'politics of mass extermination' (2021, p. 18). Nearly one million Indigenous Algerians (out of a total population of three million) were killed in the French colonizing war between 1830 and 1875, some through the deliberate mass asphyxiations known as *enfumades* (Jarvis, 2021, pp. 3, 18, citing Lazali, 2018). As many as a million more Algerians died in the struggle for independence (known by Algerians as *al-thawra*, or revolution), which was led by the Front de Libération Nationale (National Liberation Front, FLN) and brutally suppressed by the French colonial army. The French state's long failure to reckon with or even recognize this history can be seen in the fact that it was not until 2018 that a French head of state acknowledged France's responsibility for the torture of Algerian fighters in the war of independence (Jarvis, 2021, pp. 10–11; Al-Jazeera, 2018).

94 'A Comparative Literature of Imperialism'

Camus is one of Said's prime examples of an author whose support for empire limits the purview of his work, a claim that goes against his frequent depiction as a universal writer who is concerned with the existential predicament of man and the human condition. Said cites Camus' opposition to the Algerian liberation struggle – which he sees as evidence of the latter's assumption of the inherent undesirability of Arab Muslim majority rule – and his acceptance of the representational 'conventions shaped in the long tradition of colonial writing on Algeria' (1994, p. 180). Djebar, on the other hand, was an Algerian Muslim from an Arab and Amazigh background (the Amazigh people or Imazighen, sometimes referred to by outsiders as Berbers, are Indigenous North Africans, predating the Arabs who arrived in the seventh century). As a young woman, she was actively involved in the Algerian national liberation struggle as a journalist for the FLN's newspaper. Her writing not only exposes French colonial crimes but also criticizes the Algerian state after independence, particularly its failure to extend the promise of liberation to Algerian women, in keeping with Frantz Fanon's insistence that true decolonization requires opposition to oppressive postcolonial regimes (cf. Gopal, 2021, pp. 881–2). Her work thus tells a story that Camus' text cannot. Reading them together makes it possible to identify the gaps and omissions in Camus' account, while also making it clear what Algerians were up against, both before and after independence.

Camus' writing about Algeria is often concerned with the profound alienation of the French settlers and their descendants. His characters feel out of place in Algeria, but they know no other home. They are sometimes aware of their unfair privilege under colonial rule, but they are wary of Algerian Muslims and unable to imagine a more just way of organizing Algerian society. The protagonist Janine in 'La femme adultère' exemplifies this predicament. The story is set not long after the Second World War, in the Algerian desert. Janine's sense of alienation from this setting is signalled early in the story, when her driver 'fire[s] off a few words in that tongue she had heard all her life without understanding'

'A Comparative Literature of Imperialism'   95

(Camus, 2006 [1957], p. 4). This is an important moment: after several pages narrating her misery on the journey, her sense of distance from her husband Marcel, and her physical discomfort, the reader suddenly gets a historical explanation for her unhappiness instead of a narrowly personal or psychological one. We are reminded that Janine has spent her life as a white French woman in a majority Arab/Amazigh Muslim country, and she does not speak Arabic or Tamazight.

To be fair, Camus often seems more aware of this colonial context than Said gives him credit for. There are several points in the story in which Janine seems to stand in for imperial France in an explicitly allegorical way. For example, when Janine and Marcel climb to the top of a fort and look down at the land and people beneath them, Janine thinks about what she sees in the language of colonial possession:

> Homeless, remote from the world, they were a handful of men wandering through *the vast territory her gaze had discovered*, and which was nonetheless only a trivial part of a still greater space ... Janine did not know why this idea filled her with a sadness so sweet and so vast that she closed her eyes. She knew only that *this kingdom had been promised to her from time immemorial*, and that it would never be hers, never again. (Camus, 2006, pp. 11–12; emphasis added)

Janine's passivity and misery in the story thus far is interrupted by an energizing sense that she has discovered the territory before her. She can see for herself that this isn't true: the people she sees on the plain make it clear that someone else was there first. But she nevertheless feels as if she can possess the territory through her gaze and is overwhelmed by the fear of losing it, an observation that once again points to the historical context of Janine's emotions. The story does not directly mention the national liberation struggle's challenge to French rule, but the language of the passage strongly evokes it.

In the story's final scene, Janine returns to the fort on her own in the middle of the night and experiences an

96   'A Comparative Literature of Imperialism'

unmistakeably sexual encounter with the land: 'with an unbearable sweetness, the waters of the night began to fill Janine, submerging the cold, rising gradually to the dark centre of her being, and overflowing wave upon wave to her moaning mouth' (Camus, 2006, p. 16). Said is scornful of Camus' apparent suggestion in this scene that Janine is able to achieve a direct communion with the earth and sky, as if she too is a native Algerian (Said, 1994, p. 177). But it's worth considering whether the reader should take this moment of communion at face value. Throughout the story, the reader never steps outside of Janine's consciousness; the narrative remains narrowly confined within her desire to possess the land. But that doesn't mean that Janine's point of view is the same as that of Camus. Perhaps Camus is more critical of Janine's desire for dominance than Said allows, or perhaps he wants to signal a less violent way for French settlers in Algeria to express their identity as Algerians, one that will require them to think of Algeria, not France, as their shared home with other Algerians.

This understanding of the story is only possible if we read it in relation to empire, not as a decontextualized account of the protagonist's pursuit of 'une certaine vie libre et nue' (a certain free and bare life), as Camus admittedly invited his readers to do (Said, 1994, p. 177). However, just as Coetzee and Rhys's identification of the omissions of the colonial record can only take us so far, it is insufficient to point out the ambivalences or limitations of Camus' writing in isolation. Decolonizing literary studies requires us to challenge Camus' view of Algeria with texts written by formerly colonized Algerians such as Djebar. This is not to say that Djebar's perspective represents that of all Algerians: she received an elite French-language education in Algiers and Paris, wrote in French, and spent much of her adult life in France and later the United States. She is also a highly celebrated figure in both French and world literature, who until her death was regularly cited as a possible winner of the Nobel Prize for Literature.[13] (Had she won, she would have been only the second Arab writer to do so, after the Egyptian novelist Naguib Mahfouz in 1988. There have

'A Comparative Literature of Imperialism' 97

been sixteen winners from France, including Camus himself in 1957.) Nevertheless, her work starkly challenges Camus' privileging of the perspectives of the French settler class, focusing instead on the violent subjugation of Algerians, especially Algerian women, during and after empire. Indeed, Djebar's writing can itself be read as contrapuntal, for she 'cram[s] her texts with literary and cultural references from all over the world' (Hiddleston, 2006, p. 13), above all the French, Arabic, and Tamazight written and oral traditions that comprise Algeria's multilingual literary heritage.[14] Like the Caribbean writers discussed in chapter 3, she faced the challenge of narrating Algerian history in French, which was the only language she could write in. This is true of many Algerian and other North African writers of her generation – including Tahar Ben Jelloun, Mohammad Dib, and Albert Memmi, to name just a few – but Djebar's work stages this dilemma especially self-consciously, calling attention to the irresolvable conflict between colonizer and colonized (like Césaire) as well as their historical and cultural inseparability.

Djebar's collection *Femmes d'Alger dans leur appartement* takes its title from an 1834 painting by Eugène Delacroix that purported to represent the woman-only space of the harem at an acquaintance's home. In the essay 'Regard interdit, son coupé' ('Forbidden gaze, severed sound'), Djebar writes of this painting:

> Nothing can be guessed about the soul of these doleful figures, seated as if drowning in all that surrounds them. They remain absent to themselves, to their body, to their sensuality, to their happiness.
> Between them and us, the spectators, there has been the instant of unveiling, the step that crossed the vestibule of intimacy, the unexpected slight touch of the thief, the spy, the voyeur. (Djebar, 1992 [1980], p. 137)

Djebar is concerned with the epistemic violence of Delacroix's act of representation and with the pleasure that the viewer is encouraged to take from their imprisonment and their

98   'A Comparative Literature of Imperialism'

silence. However, the Orientalizing gaze of the French painter is not the only target of her critique. On the next page, she claims that this silencing of women, of turning them into objects of the gaze, is also practised by Algerian men in independent Algeria:

> That particular gaze had long been believed to be a stolen one because it was the stranger's, the one from outside the harem and outside the city.
>
> For a few decades – as each nationalism triumphs here and there – we have been able to realize that within this Orient that has been delivered unto itself, the image of woman is still perceived no differently, be it by the father, by the husband, and, more troublesome still, by the brother and the son. (Djebar, 1992, p. 138)

Djebar alludes here to the betrayal of the fight for women's liberation by the men who were supposed to champion it: the 'brothers' of the national liberation struggle and the future generations of liberated 'sons'. Much of Djebar's writing seeks to represent Algerian women's resistance to these connected forms of patriarchal oppression. Her multifaceted critique can be seen clearly in an early story in *Femmes d'Alger*, 'Il n'y a pas d'exil' ('There is no exile'), written in Tunisia in 1959. In this story, Djebar's nameless narrator is imprisoned by many different structures: her forced exile outside of Algeria, her confinement to an apartment, her grief at the deaths of her two young children in the war, and the institution of marriage, which is the only future that her family can see for her. But, at the same time, the narrator also fiercely expresses her resistance. The female relatives of her prospective husband come to the apartment to inspect her, to gaze at her, but she gazes back:

> I raised my head: it was then, I think, that *I met Hafsa's gaze*. There was, deep in her eyes, a strange light, surely of interest or irony, I don't know, but you could feel Hafsa as an outsider, attentive and curious at the same time, but an outsider. *I met that look.*

'A Comparative Literature of Imperialism'   99

'I don't want to marry,' I said. 'I don't want to marry,' I repeated, barely shouting. (Djebar, 1992, p. 71; emphasis added)

In this scene, the character Hafsa is a violent spectator, like Delacroix and his viewers: she is trying to impose her will on the protagonist, who refuses to allow this to happen. Djebar thus shares with Camus an interest in moments of freedom that are achieved through defiance of social convention and expectation, even though the political implications of their invocations of freedom are very different. In 'Regard interdit, son coupé', she famously invokes Picasso's 1955 series of paintings in response to Delacroix, which are also called *Les femmes d'Alger* but are very different in style and effect. Djebar sees Picasso's work as having opened the door of the harem and let in the light, which she associates with social and physical freedom: the women are naked, their breasts bursting out (Djebar, 1992, p. 149).[15] She draws a parallel between Picasso's paintings and the liberation sought by female bomb carriers in the Algerian national liberation struggle. Djebar observes:

It is a question of wondering whether the carriers of the bombs, as they left the harem, chose their most direct manner of expression purely by accident: their bodies exposed outside and they themselves attacking other bodies? In fact, they took these bombs out as if they were taking out their own breasts, and those grenades exploded against them, right against them. (Ibid., p. 150)

Yet these women's pursuit of freedom through physical exposure and sacrifice went unrealized. During the war, 'the whole of the Algerian collective' condemned the torture and rape that French soldiers inflicted on Algerian women fighters. But after independence the 'heavy silence' about other kinds of violence against women returned, reinstating 'the law of invisibility, the law of silence' (ibid., pp. 150–1). Djebar ends the essay, which also ends the collection, by

100   'A Comparative Literature of Imperialism'

asserting that women's liberation requires 'the door open to the full sun' (ibid., p. 151). This is a call for women to tell their own stories, for them to be heard as widely as possible, and for the patriarchal structures that keep them silent and abused to be destroyed. Algerian women writers who have come after Djebar, such as Maïssa Bey (Samia Benameur), Rabia Djelti, Yamina Méchakra, Ahlam Mosteghanemi, Samira Negrouche, Zahia Rahmani, and Leila Sebbar, take up her call.[16] These authors write in French and Arabic, sometimes drawing on one or more Amazigh languages, from a range of locations (in Algeria, France, and elsewhere) and a range of political positions. Their works challenge the French state's amnesia about its colonial terror in Algeria, the Algerian state's co-optation of revolutionary memory and use of violence to maintain power, and Algerian political Islamists' anti-secularism and anti-feminism, continuing the ongoing struggle for women's liberation and the unfinished business of decolonization.

Both writing back and contrapuntal reading can be understood as a way of reclaiming multiple voices in history, excavating alternative histories and knowledge, and considering the relationships between them. As Gopal points out, 'decolonisation is not a matter of relativising these [overlooked insights] alongside received knowledge but of putting them in dialogue' (2021, p. 895). This comparative approach to reading colonial and anticolonial texts insists that we 'interpret both sides of the contest not only hermeneutically but also politically' (Said, 1994, p. 259). In other words, we must not simply describe what these texts do but align ourselves with the struggle for decolonization that they reject or defend. The next chapter, by prioritizing texts that explicitly seek to contribute to anticolonial political movements, considers a way of deepening and extending the political commitment that contrapuntal reading calls for.

Summary

- Unlike 'writing back', which describes a kind of writing, contrapuntal criticism is a strategy for reading. It holds that we must read texts with different relationships to empire comparatively in order to grasp the role that European empire has played in the making of the entire world.
- Albert Camus and Assia Djebar both depict colonial (and, in Djebar's case, postcolonial) Algeria, but they do so from very different standpoints. Camus examines the anxieties and alienation of French settlers in Algeria, while Djebar focuses on the experiences of colonized Algerians before and after independence, particularly Algerian women.
- While Said in *Culture and Imperialism* accuses Camus of uncritically deploying tropes of colonial writing, Camus' short story 'La femme adultère' seems conscious of the protagonist's colonial sensibilities. However, it stops short of challenging them or offering an alternative perspective.
- Djebar's work offers an alternative to that of Camus through its emphasis on Algerian women's oppression and resistance before, during, and after the national liberation struggle against France. She celebrates moments of women's resistance and calls for an end to the silence that surrounds their violent subjugation.
- Reading these texts together puts their arguments and ideas into dialogue. It challenges the gaps and omissions of Camus' account while also showing what colonized Algerians were up against, and it demands that the reader choose a side.

–5–

Telling a Collective Story: Literature and Anticolonial Struggle

As I have argued in previous chapters, diversifying the literature curriculum is only a first step in decolonizing literary studies as a discipline. This means that, while attention to writers' geographical, ethnic, class, and gender identities is indispensable, it is just part of the task of rethinking what and how we read. This chapter proposes that we also attend to writers' political affiliations, focusing on how writers who expressly conceive of their work as part of an organized movement seek to persuade and inspire their readers. The first part of the chapter discusses work by participants in key anticolonial struggles of the mid-twentieth century (1960s–1970s), considering autobiographies by Leila Khaled (Palestine), Doris Tijerino Haslam (Nicaragua), and Angela Davis (United States). The second part turns to two contemporary activist battlegrounds: the transnational environmental movement and the struggle for migrant and refugee rights, examining non-fiction works by Arundhati Roy (India) and Behrouz Boochani (Iran/Australia/New Zealand).

These texts demand to be read as contributions to a collective struggle, which makes them difficult to interpret with the standard tools of literary criticism and pedagogy (reading for the subtext, for 'universal' themes, for language play, and so on). This chapter examines some of their key

Telling a Collective Story 103

techniques, including how they address their readers, their use of specifically anticolonial and anti-capitalist vocabulary and imagery, and their deployment of a proleptic mode of narration, through which they anticipate the future victory of their struggle. It also considers the contemporary writers' responses to the challenge of persuading their readers at a time when a language of political sincerity risks being seen as outdated or naïve, foregrounding their efforts to revive and transform revolutionary discourse for our present moment.

I'm aware that some readers of this book may struggle to think of the works considered in this chapter as properly 'literary'. They belong to the non-fictional genres of life writing, journalism, and essay (rather than fiction, poetry, or drama, like most of the other texts I address); they are often overt, even didactic, in their tone and argument; and some are unlikely to be read after the struggle they promote has ended. In what follows, I invite readers to try to set these reactions aside and, instead, to think of the texts' features as literary techniques that are worthy of contemplation and criticism in themselves. This means taking seriously Barbara Harlow's claim that '[t]he theory of resistance literature is in its politics' (1987, p. 30; see also chapter 1) by centring these texts' political intentions and effects in our readings.

Reflection I: Literature as political persuasion

1. What are the main sources of your political ideas and education? Has literature contributed to the formation of your political beliefs? Why or why not?
2. Have you ever read a literary text that has changed your mind about an issue? If so, what made that text have that effect on you?
3. What persuasive tactics would you expect to see in a text that seeks to educate its reader and/or change their opinion? What stylistic techniques do you think such a text might use?

104 Telling a Collective Story

4. Would you rather that a text that seeks to change your mind make its argument subtly or explicitly? Why?
5. In general, do you think contemporary readers in your location are receptive to explicitly political texts? Why or why not? Who do you think the readership for such texts is (as opposed to other kinds of political outreach)? Who gets included, and who is left out?

Liberation struggles of the 1960s and 1970s: women's autobiographies

The authors discussed in this section are linked not only by their shared historical moment and their identity as women but also by their importance in their respective movements. Leila Khaled is a member of Al-Jabhah al-Shabiyyah li-Tahrir Filastin (Popular Front for the Liberation of Palestine, PFLP), a Palestinian revolutionary socialist organization. She became internationally famous for her role in two PFLP aeroplane hijackings in 1969 and 1970, when 'her image joined that of [Argentinian revolutionary] Che Guevara on thousands of left-wing walls' (Irving, 2012, p. 6). She has since held senior roles in the PFLP, including serving as a representative of the party in the General Union of Palestinian Women and on the Palestinian National Council (ibid., p. 87). Doris Tijerino is a member of the Frente Sandinista de Liberación Nacional (Sandinista National Liberation Front, FSLN), founded in the 1960s to free Nicaragua from the rule of the US-backed dictator Anastasio Somoza, whose family had ruled the country since 1936. The FSLN overthrew Somoza in 1979 and formed their own government, which remained in power until their electoral defeat in 1990. Their priorities in government included land redistribution, national literacy, unionization, and women's equality.[17] Tijerino was a movement leader and combatant who was imprisoned and

Telling a Collective Story 105

brutally tortured multiple times during the liberation struggle in the 1960s and 1970s. Once the FSLN assumed power, she became the general secretary of their women's association, the Asociación de Mujeres Nicaragüenses Luisa Amanda Espinoza (AMNLAE), and later served as the national chief of police and a member of the Nicaraguan Parliament. Angela Davis is a Black American scholar and leading member of the US Black liberation movement and previously (until 1991) the US Communist Party. Unlike Khaled and Tijerino, she has not participated in armed struggle, but in 1970 she was arrested and jailed because a gun registered in her name had been used in a courtroom attack in California, in which the presiding judge and the three attackers were killed. Many supporters believed that Davis was deliberately targeted for her activism and political affiliations. The campaign to free her received widespread attention, and like Khaled she became an iconic figure of the international left. She was acquitted in a jury trial in 1972 and has since continued her work as a political organizer, speaker, and university professor.

Khaled, Tijerino, and Davis all published autobiographies in English shortly after the events the texts depict, with the explicit aim of furthering the ongoing struggle. Khaled's *My People Shall Live* (1973) was published in London, as told to George Hajjar, a Lebanese-Canadian academic who then worked for the PFLP publicity department in Beirut (Irving, 2012, p. 3). The book circulated widely: it was also published in Canada – though not the United States – and translated into Arabic, Pashto, Japanese, German, and French. Although it has long been out of print, it continues to reach new readers in pdf form online (ibid., p. 71). Tijerino's autobiography, as told to the US academic and activist Margaret Randall, was first published in Mexico under the title *Somos millones: la vida de Doris María, combatiente nicaragüense* (We are millions: the life of Doris María, Nicaraguan fighter, 1977). When Tijerino was captured once again in 1978, Randall and other comrades feared that she would be killed and so worked to get the English translation published quickly to raise international awareness of her

106   Telling a Collective Story

imprisonment (Byron, 2006, p. 114). The English translation appeared with the Canadian activist press New Star Books as *Inside the Nicaraguan Revolution* (1978). Like Khaled's book, it was never reissued by a US press, and it is now out of print. Finally, Angela Davis's *An Autobiography* was first published in 1974 – in this case, by the major New York publisher Random House – and quickly translated into ten other languages, including Hungarian, Slovenian, and Japanese, demonstrating the reach of the international campaign for her release. Like Khaled's autobiography, it sought to mobilize Davis's global visibility to raise awareness of the wider struggle for equality and justice for Black Americans. A new edition, with a new introduction by the author, was published by Haymarket Books and Penguin in 2022, indicating Davis's continuing stature in the Black liberation struggle in the United States and beyond.[18]

The literary critic Margo Perkins, in a discussion of Davis's autobiography alongside those of her contemporaries Assata Shakur and Elaine Brown, observes that, while scholarly accounts of the US Black liberation movement draw on women's autobiographies as resources for writing movement histories, they usually fail to analyse them '*as texts*', for instance by considering *how* they 'fill in, complement, challenge, or converse with the stories told by their male counterparts' (Perkins, 2000, pp. 10–11). This oversight also happens in literary studies, but for different reasons: political autobiographies are rarely analysed 'as texts' (or indeed at all) because they fail to conform to a narrow definition of what literature is. (Exceptions include works such as Barbara Harlow's *Resistance Literature*, discussed in chapter 1, as well as her subsequent work on assassinated writers [1996].) Yet if one believes, as I do, that decolonizing literary studies compels us to return to the 'radical *theorizing* of decolonization' (Wenzel, 2017; see also chapter 1) of the mid-twentieth century, this means that texts that expressly seek to contribute to the anticolonial struggles of that period are required reading. The social visions that these texts articulate, the state violence they document and resist, and the organizational setbacks and successes they depict contribute

Telling a Collective Story 107

not only to our understanding of the history of anticolonial thought but also to its possible futures. To approach the autobiographies of Khaled, Tijerino, and Davis 'as texts' is to consider both what they say and how they say it, and also to think about what it might mean to see literature's contribution to anticolonial struggle as its most important attribute.

One of these texts' major shared features is how they approach the genre of autobiography itself. Each text repeatedly asserts that the narrator's experiences should be seen not as exceptional but, rather, as representative of and subordinate to the wider struggle. This claim upends a key assumption of the European life writing canon: namely, that the protagonist is in some way unusual or exemplary. Yet it also creates a provocative tension between the narrator's status as a hero of her movement (which is presumably what would attract many readers to these texts in the first place) and her insistence that she is an ordinary participant. This tension is especially pronounced in Khaled's *My People Shall Live*. For instance, in the final chapter she recounts having undergone plastic surgery so that she could carry out a second hijacking without being recognized, after her first hijacking had made her internationally famous. Khaled describes the operation as follows:

> It was extremely painful. Since I was refused a general anaesthetic, I could see as well as feel the thrust of the needles. I suppose people in the West will conclude that I must be a masochist, but I assure them that I am not. I have a cause higher and nobler than my own, a cause to which all private interests and concerns must be subordinated. Hence I lay on the operating table while my comrades were being tortured, my sisters being raped and my land pillaged. (Khaled, 1973, p. 180)

What is striking about this passage is the speed at which Khaled moves from the matter-of-fact statement of her own physical pain – something that the reader might expect a memoir to dwell on – to a reminder of the wider struggle

108 Telling a Collective Story

that motivates it. She registers her suffering, but she presents it as unremarkable compared to the mass agony of the Palestinian population and refuses to make an exception of her own bravery or sacrifice. She also anticipates and rejects an imagined 'Western' reader's erroneous reading of the scene in terms of her individual psychology by insisting that her action stems from her political convictions. She then follows the rather abstract invocation of a 'higher and nobler' cause with the more emotive sequence of the words 'tortured', 'raped', and 'pillaged', conveying a ruthless and excessive violence that the reader should join her in opposing.

The impassioned narrative register that Khaled employs in this passage appears at times in all three texts. However, it is most noticeable in Khaled's, particularly in the dramatic sequence of events that follows her surgery: the hijacking is foiled, she is captured, and her Nicaraguan-American comrade Patrick Argüello is killed.[19] Khaled eulogizes Argüello in effusive terms, connecting his individual heroism to the wider Palestinian movement and to other anticolonial liberation struggles: 'you have joined Che [Guevara] in revolutionary love. You are an inspiration for the weak and oppressed. The Palestinians shall build you monuments in their hearts and in their liberated homeland' (Khaled, 1973, p. 191). For the reader who has been trained to view sincerity and directness as non- or extra-literary traits, in keeping with what Timothy Brennan calls the 'modernist literary dominant' (2017, p. 267; see also chapters 1 and 6), it might be difficult to recognize Khaled's vocabulary and tone as stylistic devices. Yet this reorientation is crucial to our ability to grasp the intellectual and artistic contributions made by the literature of decolonization struggles. Khaled's mode of expression sets out to encourage and strengthen the reader's support for the Palestinian national liberation movement; this purpose is integral to the narrative and cannot be conceived separately from it. Her style might be understood as an aesthetic expression of what David Featherstone describes as the 'embodied passionate character of connections' between participants in a political movement (2012, p. 36). Its heightened emotional register asserts the

Telling a Collective Story

struggle's importance and urges the reader to share the narrator's emotions. Tijerino's autobiography generally employs a more modulated tone than Khaled's, but it similarly affirms the inseparability of her life story from her involvement in the struggle for Nicaraguan national liberation. As in Khaled's and Davis's texts, much of the early part of Tijerino's narrative is taken up with the story of her political education. This is in keeping with the conventions of the political autobiography, to employ a term that Davis uses to describe her own narrative (Davis, 2022 [1974]; cf. Perkins, 2000, p. 20). Such works implicitly or explicitly offer the story of the narrator's political education as an analogy for the reader's: the reader is invited to learn alongside the narrator and undergo a parallel process of coming to political awareness. Tijerino's point of view at the start of the narrative is comparable to the reader's in part because of her privileged upbringing: her family were landowners and she received a full primary and secondary education. She narrates her feelings of shock and shame as she comes to realize the conditions of extreme poverty endured by many of her fellow Nicaraguans, who subsist on hard manual labour for minimal pay without access to education or healthcare. Her stories of the lack of medical care are especially harrowing. She recounts stories of a woman and her baby who died in childbirth because the landowners were attending the birth of a calf and a man who nearly died after cutting himself with a machete while working in the fields (Tijerino and Randall, 1978, pp. 29–31), as well as an unnecessary death that she personally witnessed: 'Once I saw a tubercular woman die in the atrium of the Matagalpa cathedral' (ibid., p. 41).

Tijerino thus invites the reader to construct a picture of the country's socio-economic landscape just as she did herself as a child and young adult and, like her, to come to see revolution as the only way to end the gross injustices of the ruling order. She does not present herself as representative of the suffering population: on the contrary, she acknowledges her class position and her need to unlearn the idea that inequality is part of the natural order of things (a

110 Telling a Collective Story

view represented by her father, who benefits from the Somoza regime). She also cites Marxist thought, particularly Maxim Gorky's novel of the build-up to the Russian revolution, *The Mother* (1906), which was given to her by her own mother; her membership of the Jovenes Socialistas (Young Socialists); and a trip to Moscow as cementing her decision to join the Sandinistas and take up arms:

> I began to have a fighting spirit and an organized and direct participation. I had a chance to bind myself organically to the country's working class. I was able to meet revolutionaries of other nations who influenced my life. I had greater access to Marxist literature, which made me understand the true role of the Party of the working class, and gave me a very clear picture of my part in the struggle. (Tijerino and Randall, 1978, pp. 65–6)

This passage, and others like it, makes it clear that Tijerino's early recognition of the suffering of other Nicaraguans was only the first step in her political education. In order to contribute effectively to the revolutionary struggle, she first had to be able to situate it in the context of the global struggle against capitalism: this meant studying Marxist texts, learning from her fellow revolutionaries, and being able to recognize the importance of the struggle intellectually as well as emotionally.

This rather cerebral account of Tijerino's political formation is similar in tone to the matter-of-fact description of her own torture at the hands of the Somoza regime. This testimony takes up only a few pages (Tijerino and Randall, 1978, pp. 100–5), which is far less space than she gives to accounts of the assassinations of her comrades or different methods of popular resistance. However, it constitutes the most direct evidence of the regime's ruthlessness and thus is crucial to the effort to persuade the reader that armed violence against this regime is necessary. The guards abuse Tijerino physically, sexually, and psychologically, in a failed attempt to make her give up the names of her comrades. Her

Telling a Collective Story   111

narration of this abuse is detailed but conveys little of her own suffering; it documents the regime's actions rather than her response. In this regard it reads more like legal testimony, and indeed she hints at this form of redress by noting that she was later able to identify in court some guards who had stood in a circle and tossed her around between them (ibid., p. 103). But elsewhere in the narrative, and particularly when she seeks to evoke a future after the fall of the Somoza regime, Tijerino's narrative takes on a more lyrical tone. This can be seen vividly in the final lines of the text, which link her early recognition of the suffering of others to her vision of the Sandinistas' future victory:

> Now I'm thinking about my childhood. About the countryside. About the peasants who died giving birth and those who died of hunger, exploitation, and misery.[20]
>
> I'm thinking about the women in jail, the peasant-prostitute, the worker-thief.
>
> I'm thinking about my own mother and her unfinished struggle.
>
> About our fallen comrades and those who are still alive.
>
> We'll keep on struggling [Seguimos luchando]. So someday all our people will dream in colour. (Tijerino and Randall, 1978, p. 164; Tijerino and Randall, 1977, p. 84)

Here Tijerino moves from documenting what the Sandinistas are fighting against to an invocation of what they are fighting for: the chance to 'dream in colour' (sueñe en colores). This is more than survival; this is a vision of a life that is worth living.

Davis's *An Autobiography* opens with an equally rousing juxtaposition of the injustice that her movement strives to end with the better future it seeks to bring about. Explaining why she reluctantly decided to write an autobiography, she says that she came to believe that such a book might make a concrete contribution to the struggle:

112   Telling a Collective Story

There was the possibility that, having read it, more people would understand why so many of us have no alternative but to offer our lives – our bodies, our knowledge, our will – to the cause of our oppressed people. In this period when the covers camouflaging the corruption and racism of the highest political offices are rapidly falling away, when the bankruptcy of the global system of capitalism is becoming apparent, there was the possibility that more people – Black, Brown, Red, Yellow and white – might be inspired to join our growing community of struggle. Only if this happens will I consider this project to have been worthwhile. (Davis, 2022)

Here, Davis offers an unapologetically instrumentalist understanding of what her narrative is for: the expansion of the Black liberation movement, which she presents as part of the global struggle against capitalism. This formulation of her aims serves as a tactic of persuasion in itself: it appeals to the reader to act in response to what they are about to read, to help ensure that her efforts will not have been in vain. This invitation expressly includes all her readers, of all racial backgrounds, in keeping with her insistence throughout the book that the struggle against racial capitalism[21] implicates us all. Her rhetoric in this passage is heightened in a different way to Khaled's. It also seeks to rouse the reader's emotions, but it does so by invoking the urgency of the struggle and the possibility of its triumph.

Davis's autobiography is also notable for its attention to the specifics of movement organizing. This subject matter is shared by all three texts, but Davis offers the fullest account of the aims, activities, and debates within and among the organizations she worked with, including the Communist Party, the Student Nonviolent Coordinating Committee (SNCC), and the Black Panther Party. (This greater emphasis might have something to do with the fact that Davis is the sole author of her narrative, while the content of Khaled's and Tijerino's texts is mediated by their collaborators.) While she criticizes some of the actions and positions these groups took, the overall tone of her narrative is celebratory,

Telling a Collective Story 113

focusing on their achievements in the face of unrelenting state surveillance, incarceration, and violence. These successes include the establishment of a Liberation School providing community political education in Los Angeles, the campaign to exonerate the political prisoners known as the Soledad Brothers, and the campaign for her own release on bail. Of the latter campaign, Davis writes that, while she had initially opposed it because bail 'was not a revolutionary demand', she came to understand that the action was effective because it engaged so many people, who then began to 'evolve politically' by coming to see the prison and judicial systems as fundamentally repressive (Davis, 2022). In this regard, Davis's narrative functions as both a source of political education (like the initiatives and campaigns she discusses) and a manual for continuing the struggle, through its assessment of the activities that were most successful in raising public awareness and building support for a mass movement.

This guidance is offered overtly: when Davis wants the reader to learn something from a particular episode, she says what the lesson is. For instance, in her account of the early period of her imprisonment, her story of the prisoners' attempts to protect themselves from the mice in the cells moves from documentation of their living conditions to a broader political analogy:

> our daily struggles with [the mice ...] were symbolic of a larger struggle with the system. Indulging in a flight of fancy, I would sometimes imagine that all the preparations that were made at night to ward off those creatures were the barricades being erected against that larger enemy. That hundreds of women, all over the jail, politically conscious, politically committed, were acting in revolutionary unison. (Davis, 2022)

Davis repeatedly models this kind of big-picture thinking for the reader, as an example of the work of visualizing collective resistance that anticolonial struggle requires. This kind of didacticism can also be seen in her frequent reminders that her experiences must be seen as representative rather than exceptional. Although a recent reading of the autobiography apologetically calls this approach 'rather emphatic' (Linke, 2019, p. 302), I suggest instead that we appreciate it as a deliberate form of pedagogy, through which Davis seeks to present her ideas as clearly as possible. This sense of educational and political purpose can be seen again in the final lines of the epilogue, where she appeals directly to the reader to support the struggle. Listing the names of currently imprisoned people, she ends with the pronouncement: 'We – you and I – are their only hope for life and freedom' (Davis, 2022).[22] This is the only moment in the text where she addresses the reader in the second person. It is significant that this moment comes at the end of the text, as the reader is about to put down the book and is at risk of not taking any further action. Davis includes the reader in the resistant collective 'we' that has the power to free these activists and insists that the reader can help bring about the future victory of the wider struggle.

> ### Reflection II: Reading texts from earlier decolonization struggles
>
> 1. What can we learn from reading texts that come out of moments in struggles that are either in the past or now take very different forms? What might they tell us about our present moment?
> 2. Does the language and reasoning of the texts discussed in this section seem outdated to you? Why or why not?
> 3. If you were trying to convince a publisher to reissue an out-of-print text such as Khaled's or Tijerino's, how would you explain its contemporary relevance?
> 4. In what ways can a return to texts from mid-century decolonization struggles inform contemporary efforts to decolonize literary studies? What kinds of ideas or structures can these texts challenge or help us to see differently?

Writing from contemporary social movements: renewing resistance in the twenty-first century

While some of the features of the mid-twentieth-century narratives I have been discussing can be seen in texts that seek to contribute to contemporary movements, the defeat of many anticolonial and anti-capitalist struggles in the intervening decades means that contemporary writers are responding to very different historical and political conditions. Although the language of revolution and resistance has taken on a new currency in the wake of the global financial collapse of 2008 and the subsequent popular uprisings of the 'Arab Spring', Los Indignados, Black Lives Matter, Occupy Wall Street, and more, the sense of political possibility and optimism that was prevalent in the era of mass decolonization remains significantly diminished. This means that the vocabulary of passionate commitment and assurance of future triumph that characterize the texts discussed above can seem naïve or old-fashioned to contemporary readers, whose political sensibilities are shaped by the imperial restoration of power that has been ongoing since the 1970s (see also my Introduction).

The writers I discuss in this section, Arundhati Roy and Behrouz Boochani, seek to revive and transform the discourse of revolutionary resistance for our present moment. Unlike Khaled and Tijerino, they do not directly advocate armed struggle, and unlike Davis they do not offer much detail of the operations of contemporary activist movements. They are also first and foremost writers rather than fighters or political organizers. However, they share with their predecessors the aim of understanding and exposing the oppressive systems that inflict violence and suffering from an anticolonial and anti-capitalist perspective. In different ways, they each offer a robust defence of the contribution that literature can make to movement politics and, conversely, highlight the need for writers to bring catastrophes such as environmental devastation and the mass detention of migrants to the attention of a broad public.

116   Telling a Collective Story

This effort can be considered a project of translation, as Rob Nixon observes of Roy's influential writing about the Sardar Sarovar mega-dam in Gujarat, India: Roy translates 'technocratic discourse' into accessible language, internationalizes a local resistance movement, and connects the destructiveness of mega-dam projects to neoliberal forms of governance everywhere (Nixon, 2011, p. 171). Boochani does something similar in his acclaimed autobiographical narrative *No Friend but the Mountains* (2018), which narrates his experience of being a prisoner in the infamous Australian detention centre on Manus Island. His implied readers are citizens of countries – above all Australia, the United Kingdom, and the United States – whose governments deem some people to be 'illegal' migrants and incarcerate them as criminals. He not only makes visible the brutal treatment of the detainees – many of whom are fleeing imperial wars in places such as Iraq and Afghanistan – but also seeks to 'produce new knowledge and to construct a philosophy that unpacks and exposes systematic torture and the border-industrial complex' (Tofighian in Boochani, 2018b, p. 372), meaning the lucrative partnership between private security companies and the governments of core capitalist countries.

Significantly, although both writers emphasize the humanity of the people they write about, they are sceptical of the language of human rights, which had until recently largely replaced the idea of revolution in the political imaginary of much of the metropolitan left (Moyn, 2010). Roy (2014) condemns the institutional 'industry of human rights' for promoting 'an atrocity-based analysis in which the larger picture can be blocked out and both parties in a conflict ... [can] be admonished as Human Rights Violators' and insists instead on the need for 'radical confrontation' of structural oppression. Boochani, meanwhile, celebrates the Manus Island detainees' uprising against their confinement, which he says transformed their humanitarian representation 'as passive actors and weak subjects into active agents and fierce resistors' (2018a, pp. 17–18). These two very different writers thus share with their mid-twentieth-century predecessors an

Telling a Collective Story 117

emphasis on systemic critique and the celebration of popular resistance instead of the language of victimhood.

Arundhati Roy grew up in the Indian states of Kerala and Tamil Nadu. She moved to Delhi, where she still lives, to attend university and subsequently worked as a screenwriter. She first came to international prominence with the publication of her novel *The God of Small Things* (1997), which received a £500,000 advance and went on to win the Booker Prize for fiction. The novel's success was due in part to the growing metropolitan market demand for Indian writing in English (discussed in chapter 3). Unlike most of her contemporaries, however, Roy took advantage of her newfound celebrity not to write more novels – she has only written one since, *The Ministry of Utmost Happiness* (2017) – but to establish herself as a political activist, essayist, and public speaker. Her non-fiction takes on government collusion with corporations, particularly in India; US imperialism; environmental justice; Indigenous activism in India, most famously the armed resistance of Maoist revolutionaries; and grassroots resistance to neoliberal capitalism. At the time of writing, she has published twenty volumes of essays and interviews, and there are tens of thousands of recordings of her speeches and interviews available online. This mobilization of her celebrity as a novelist has given Roy a new kind of 'insurgent' celebrity (Nayar, 2017) among the international left, making her a 'primary invigorating voice for a whole new generation of antiglobalization activists' (Nixon, 2011, p. 171). Yet Roy's activist writing has received much less scholarly attention than her fiction and also more negative attention, with some scholars lamenting her turn from the novel to the essay (e.g. Mullaney, 2002; Baneth-Nouailhetas, 2008, p. 103). This rejection is symptomatic of the general critical failure to engage with the form and style of explicitly political work that I have pointed out previously. Roy's essays are just as much a product of literary craft as her fiction and deserve equal attention to their technique.

The form and style of Roy's essays should be understood first in relation to the tradition of anticolonial internationalist reportage, a journalistic tradition featuring eyewitness accounts by socialist writers (Majumder, 2020, p. 143; Varma, 2021, pp. 368–75). It became widespread in the 1920s and 1930s, after the establishment of the Soviet Union and at the height of the international communist movement.[23] A key way in which Roy echoes this tradition is by urging her reader to take sides, as she observes in a 2001 talk on a US university campus: 'I make it clear that I think it's right and moral to take that position, and what's even worse, I use everything in my power to flagrantly solicit support for that position' (Roy, 2016). Perhaps the most 'flagrant' of her techniques of persuasion is her use of a passionately adversarial narrative voice. She wryly acknowledges her use of this tactic in a well-known 1999 essay on the Sardar Sarovar mega-dam, noting that an independent review commissioned by the World Bank condemned the project in 'temperate, measured tones (which I admire but cannot achieve)' (2016). This acerbic aside is typical of Roy's frequent use of sarcasm to mock the targets of her critique. It also points to her 'quarrel with the genre of the report' for its 'calculated opacity' and 'profoundly consequential tedium' (Nixon, 2011, pp. 168–9). The World Bank review called the mega-dam 'flawed', but it did so in a 357-page document that few outside their organization would ever read (Roy, 2016). Roy's 'translation' of such documents into plain and partisan language shows what the essay form can do for contemporary anticolonial struggle, by laying bare the cruelty and moral bankruptcy of state and international institutions' pursuit of short-term profit above all else. Roy's interweaving of 'facts, figures, and reportage with sharp political analysis' (Varma, 2021, p. 371), like the texts discussed in the previous section, thus has a clear pedagogical intent. It seeks to share information in an approachable, impassioned, and pithy style that will mobilize as many readers as possible to take action.

An attention to Roy's techniques of persuasion raises the question of who she is writing for. As Rashmi Varma notes, Roy has often published left arguments in mainstream liberal and centre-left outlets. While this has led to accusations of hypocrisy (because it suggests that many of her readers come from the ruling class she criticizes), it has also allowed her

Telling a Collective Story 119

to reach a much broader readership than if she had limited her work to more radical left publications (Varma, 2021, p. 370). A related sign of Roy's effort to address a wide audience is her use of novelistic features that might enhance her essays' appeal to readers who could be turned off by straight polemic. For instance, alongside sarcasm and other forms of humour, Roy frequently relies on 'rhetorical excess' (Rao, 2008, pp. 170–1): lists, hyperbole, alliteration, profusions of adjectives, non-standard use of capitalization, and so on, all of which also appear in her fiction. Nagesh Rao sees this novelization of the essay form as 'carnivalesque' (ibid., p. 162), a quality that he associates with the exuberance of collective resistance.

As an example, in the opening paragraphs of the title essay of *Capitalism: A Ghost Story* (2014) Roy recounts going to see Antilla, the inconceivably extravagant Mumbai residence of India's richest man, Mukesh Ambani. Roy's initial description of the house is playful: noticing the drying patches of grass on the building's twenty-seven-storey vertical lawn, she observes that '[c]learly, Trickledown hadn't worked. But Gush-Up certainly had.' 'Trickledown' refers to the discredited idea of 'trickle-down economics', which posits that tax cuts for businesses and wealthy individuals result in the creation of more jobs for middle- and lower-class workers – i.e. a 'trickling down' of wealth. Roy highlights the literal meaning of 'trickle down' by associating it with the watering of (vertical) lawns and then counters the term (capitalized to highlight its institutionalized dishonesty) with her own coinage of 'Gush-Up' to describe what actually happens to wealth under capitalism: those with capital extract wealth from other people's labour and hoard it. But Roy then adopts a more sombre tone, noting that the upper- and middle-class Indians who benefit from the current order 'live side by side with spirits of the netherworld, the poltergeists of dead rivers, dry wells, bald mountains, and denuded forests: the ghosts of 250,000 debt-ridden farmers who have killed themselves, and of the 800 million who have been impoverished and dispossessed to make room for us.' Roy's shift to a 'melodramatic and

120 Telling a Collective Story

sensational' register highlights the 'brutality of accumulation' (Comfort, 2008, p. 138) represented by Ambani's grotesque display of wealth. As in a melodrama, she clearly identifies the heroes and villains of this story. At the same time, she tries to make the scale of the mass dispossession that Antilla represents imaginable not only through numbers but also by monumentalizing it as a tragedy of epic proportions. These shifts between registers contribute to her effort to 'narrat[e] a social totality in which small stories and grand narratives shape and constitute one another', as in the realist novel (Fuchs, 2020, p. 1191).

Like the work of her mid-twentieth-century predecessors, Roy's essays also often end with a rallying cry. This is particularly noticeable in pieces such as 'Speech to the people's university' (2014), in which Roy tells a group of Occupy Wall Street protestors that they have joined 'thousands of other resistance movements all over the world in which the poorest of people are standing up and stopping the richest corporations in their tracks. Few of us dreamed that we would see you, the people of the United States, on our side trying to do this in the heart of Empire.' Roy outlines here a politics of solidarity that links the centre and peripheries of the capitalist world-system. She gives her listeners a reason to continue their struggle and the reader who has not yet taken part a reason to join in. She offers a list of collective demands – the end of corporate governance by stealth; a return to public ownership of resources and infrastructure; the right to shelter, education, and healthcare; and an end to inheritance – but the speech's appeal goes beyond its refusal of the ravages of neoliberalism. Like Davis, Roy includes the listener/reader in a righteous 'we' that will one day triumph: 'our anger alone', she declares, 'would be enough to destroy them.' She invites her reader to share in the return of political optimism.

Behrouz Boochani's *No Friend but the Mountains* also offers grounds for optimism, not only in its political vision but also the context of its production, since the text itself exists because of solidarity activism. Boochani is a Kurdish-Iranian journalist who had to flee Iran in 2013 after a raid

Telling a Collective Story 121

on the offices of the magazine he co-founded, *Werya*, put him at serious risk of imprisonment and potentially death. The magazine advocated for Kurdish language and culture in the face of government suppression of the Kurdish minority in Iran, and Boochani had already previously been arrested for this work (Skilbeck in Boochani, 2018a, pp. 7–8). He travelled to Indonesia and then tried to reach Australia in a boat carrying dozens of other asylum seekers, including children. As Boochani relates in *No Friend*, the boat capsized and the surviving passengers were rescued by a British cargo ship. They were transferred to Australian state custody and then to a migrant detention centre on Manus Island (part of Papua New Guinea) run by private companies – including the British security company G4S – on behalf of the Australian government. The conditions in Manus Prison (as Boochani calls it) were abominable and the prisoners were held indefinitely. It was shut down in 2017 after the Papua New Guinean government declared it illegal and enforced its closure. However, the prisoners, who could not return to their countries of origin and had nowhere else to go, refused to leave the camps and led a three-week uprising. They were eventually forcibly removed to new accommodation – Boochani among them – and remained stranded on Manus Island.

Throughout this period, Boochani acted as a liaison between the prisoners and the outside world. He was 'the first point of contact for many Australian and international journalists' (Tofighian in Boochani, 2018b, p. 375) and collaborated with a number of Australian and Iranian writers, academics, and activists. He reported on Manus Prison in the international press; wrote for academic journals; co-directed the film *Chauka, Please Tell Us the Time* (2017), which he shot inside the prison on his phone; and participated in the Manus Recording Project Collective, an audio oral history project produced by detainees and outside supporters (Dao and Boochani, 2020). Alongside this work, he wrote *No Friend* in the form of text messages sent to his English-language translator Omid Tofighian, an Iranian-Australian academic then based at the University of Sydney.

As Tofighian observes in his afterword, Boochani wrote the book in Farsi, Iran's official language and thus 'the language of his oppressors', rather than in Kurdish; the book was then translated into English, 'the language of his jailers and torturers' (Tofighian in Boochani, 2018b, p. 394). This decision foregrounds his effort to reach readers whose governments are responsible for the immiseration he depicts. *No Friend* was published by Picador in 2018 and won both the Victorian Prize for Literature and the Victorian Premier's Prize for Non-Fiction, two prizes that had previously been open only to Australian citizens or residents. The book's foreword, by the well-known Australian novelist Richard Flanagan, pointedly refers to Boochani as a 'great Australian writer' (Boochani, 2018b). Boochani left Manus Island for New Zealand on a one-month visitor's visa in 2019 and was granted refugee status there in 2020.

No Friend but the Mountains is a difficult book to categorize. It is not exactly an autobiography: Boochani offers almost no detail of his life before his arrival in Indonesia and does not mention his work as a journalist and artist since he came to Manus, instead focusing entirely on the boat journey and the prison. It is also not just Boochani's story: it is full of vignettes of what he describes as 'composite characters', meaning that they are based on multiple people and events to protect the identities of his fellow detainees. It might thus be broadly described as 'refugee narrative', but Tofighian rejects this label on the grounds that Boochani's narrative does not seek to produce empathy but rather aims 'to hold a mirror up to the system, dismantle it, and produce a historical record to honour those who have been killed and everyone who is still suffering.' Better ways of classifying the text, Tofighian suggests, include 'clandestine philosophical literature, prison narratives, philosophical fiction, Australian dissident writing, Iranian political art, transnational literature, decolonial writing and the Kurdish literary tradition' (Tofighian in Boochani, 2018b, p. 371).

With these comments, Tofighian translates not only the language of Boochani's text but also its intellectual, political, and literary genealogies. Both men are conscious of the risk that the narrative will be received as a testimony of Boochani's experience rather than as a work of philosophy and political theory. It should be read, Tofighian argues, as an effort to communicate 'the horrors of systematic torture integral to the detention system', a subject on which detained refugees have the greatest authority (Tofighian in Boochani, 2018b, p. 362). The book rejects reductive and patronizing stereotypes of refugees as tragic, desperate, or broken (ibid., p. 365), positioning them instead as creators of knowledge that those who have not been imprisoned cannot produce. This is one of the ways in which *No Friend* participates in the project of decolonization.

Boochani's documentation of life in the prison accordingly seeks to present a total picture of the Australian detention system's interlocking systems of control (or 'kyriarchy', a term coined by Elisabeth Schüssler Fiorenza that Boochani employs throughout the book). He describes the deplorable conditions in which the prisoners are housed: in suffocatingly hot shacks, with inadequate food and the use of a toilet block whose floor is covered in a standing pool of urine and sometimes faeces, emitting a stench 'so vile that one feels ashamed to be part of the human species' (Boochani, 2018b, p. 179). Boochani identifies these conditions as essential to the system's mechanisms of control: it is 'an extremely oppressive form of governance that the prisoner internalises, a system that leaves the prisoner simply trying to cope.' It is easier to cope if one cooperates: 'it may mean there is less to endure. And this is exactly what the system is based on and is designed to accomplish' (ibid., pp. 208–9). He argues that the endless queues for food, cigarettes, and the telephone all serve as a *'raw and palpable reinforcement of torture'* (ibid., p. 193). Not only do they reduce the prisoners to their physical needs and rob them of their time and agency, but the effort to navigate these obstacles takes up all their mental energy: 'it is impossible to find a prisoner who has not struggled to unriddle the complexities of the queuing system and the food situation to which it leads. I dare say that the mind of every prisoner is caught up with these perplexities' (ibid., p. 206).

124   Telling a Collective Story

Boochani also narrates acts of physical violence against prisoners, but most of his description of the prison is taken up with this kind of forensic accounting of the devastating effects of these ostensibly non-violent everyday forms of control, which are common to all carceral systems. While he often presents this evidence and analysis in the scholarly mode I have previously quoted, the narrative also makes use of techniques from poetry and fiction. His prose is interspersed with sections of lyric poetry, a formatting decision that Tofighian says is 'faithful to the poetic elements in the language and in Behrouz's writing' (Tofighian in Boochani, 2018b, p. 387). Boochani also makes use of a narrative mode that Tofighian calls 'horrific surrealism', a key feature of the Kurdish oral and literary tradition, which foregrounds the subconscious and fuses reality with 'dreams and creative ways of re-imagining the natural environment' (ibid., pp. 366–7). The qualifier 'horrific' refers to the nightmarish quality of many of the dream sequences, which reflects the grim reality Boochani encounters. For instance, in a dream while he is asleep on the boat, he sees piles of war dead in the Kurdish mountains juxtaposed with a vision of the boat breaking apart, a fear that is then immediately realized (Boochani, 2018b, pp. 28–34). This intertextual use of form points to one of the ways in which Boochani's narrative goes beyond the effort to inform and persuade potential allies. It also situates his text in relation to the much longer history of Kurdish resistance to colonial occupation and dispossession, locating the story of Manus Prison as part of the Kurdish people's epic struggle for survival (Tofighian in Boochani, 2018b, p. 367).

Boochani's invocation of this legacy is one of the ways in which he seeks to reinvigorate older traditions of resistance for contemporary struggle. Another is his cumulative representation of his fellow prisoners as an emergent collective. Importantly, he refuses to romanticize his comrades on the grounds of their oppression. Instead, he often comments on the bad behaviour of individuals who hoard food or jump the queue or claim the best spots on the boat, observing that 'the collapse of others appeals to the oppressor in all of

Telling a Collective Story   125

us' (2018b, p. 53). But he also foregrounds their moments of camaraderie and heroism. When the boat capsizes, the passengers clinging to its wreckage give him the strength to swim to them by 'screaming support; urging me to keep fighting' (ibid., p. 40). In the prison, he offers an admiring profile of a prisoner known as Maysam the Whore, a dancer and performer who helps his fellow prisoners 'experience the essence of life' (ibid., p. 141). Another moment of heroism comes from a prisoner who resists the guards' restraints, proclaiming, 'We are all human beings. Humans caring for other humans.' He is then violently crushed to the ground, as retribution for 'the power that he took from them' (ibid., pp. 271, 276–8).

While Boochani does not expressly link these moments of inspiring solidarity and resistance to organized struggle in *No Friend*, in his manifesto 'Letter from Manus Island' he makes their political significance more explicit. He describes the prisoners' uprising as a 'completely democratic' resistance, where all decisions were made through collective discussion and supplies were shared equally among all the members of the community, including the camp dogs (Boochani, 2018a, pp. 15–16). The prisoners not only asserted their own worth as human beings but also 'return[ed] something valuable to the majority of the Australian public ... We formulated a schema of humanity that is, precisely, in polar opposition to fascist thinking – the kind of thinking that created Manus prison' (ibid., p. 20). The prisoners' resistance resonates beyond the specific circumstances of their struggle. In place of a social hierarchy that seeks to justify the brutal incarceration of human beings, they offer their realization that 'humans have no sanctuary except within other human beings ... All this violence designed in government spaces and targeted against us has driven our lives towards nature, / towards the natural environment, / towards the animal world, / towards the ecosystem' (ibid., pp. 20, 22). Boochani thus goes beyond the effort to document and expose the horrors of militarized and privatized border regimes. He offers, like the migrant activists themselves, a vision of how a truly egalitarian and sustainable society might look.

Reflection III: Movement literature today

1. What do you think makes a contemporary movement text effective? Why do you think that Roy and Boochani have drawn such a wide readership?
2. What do you make of their use of fictional techniques within their non-fiction writing? Do you think it enhances or detracts from the effectiveness of their work?
3. In an age of online activism, is there still a place for book-length texts such as Roy's and Boochani's? Why or why not?

–6–
Decolonizing Genre: Anticolonial Understandings of Literary Craft

The last chapter sought to expand our understanding of what counts as literature by attending to the form and style of works of life writing and journalism that overtly seek to politicize their readers. This chapter returns to texts that might be considered more conventionally 'literary', focusing on works by Jamaica Kincaid (Antigua/United States), Layli Long Soldier (Oglala Lakota/United States), and Dalia Taha (Palestine). This designation comes from the authors' techniques, which can broadly be described as 'modernist', and from their recognition by the metropolitan literary establishment via prizes, fellowships, and commissions. The chapter sets out to challenge another kind of common response to literature by Black and other writers of colour: it questions the institutional and popular tendency to read the work of such writers as a source of information about their background rather than as an example of literary craft whose engagement with historical and political ideas cannot be separated from the text's use of form and technique. It thus builds on the discussion in chapter 2 of the ways in which terms such as 'experimental' or 'avant-garde' are implicitly coded as 'white', and the corollary assumption that works that are explicitly concerned with race, gender, and/or other forms of identity are not experimental (De'Ath, 2019, 2020).

128 Decolonizing Genre

I am especially concerned in this chapter (as in much of the rest of this book) with these writers' creative use of form and technique in genres other than the novel. Both scholarship and classroom teaching of postcolonial and world literature have given far more attention to the novel than to other genres. This is at least partly because the novel lends itself to the provision of information about a particular place and time, thus promising to satisfy readers' expectations that, by reading (say) a novel by a Nigerian author, they will increase their knowledge of Nigerian history and culture. Unfortunately, the dominance of the novel has overshadowed other genres that might make it easier for readers to see questions of craft and style as interdependent with content. It has also obscured the fact that, in many formerly colonized places, the novel has not been the primary genre of literary production, meaning that entire traditions centred on other genres have been overlooked. As Shital Pravinchandra puts it in a discussion of the importance of the short story in South Asian languages other than English, 'genre – especially the genre-based narrative that links novel to nation – has *everything* to do with the texts that world literature scholarship deems worthy of study, and with which texts circulate in the world republic of letters' (2018, p. 208).

To counter this narrow focus on the novel, this chapter considers short stories, poetry, and plays whose anticolonial interventions depend on their inventive use of genre. Genre is not simply a method of classification: writers use it to play with their readers' expectations, deploying and unsettling generic codes and conventions. In colonial and postcolonial contexts, they may also invoke forms associated with pre-colonial indigenous cultures and with the history of anticolonial struggle alongside or against forms associated with European imperialism. I contend that thinking about genre helps us both to apprehend the impact of colonial history and anticolonial resistance on literary form and to appreciate the specific ways that literary texts make anticolonial claims. The first part of the chapter reviews some literary-critical debates about the status of canonical

Western aesthetic categories, including Western genres, in relation to that of aesthetic traditions from the rest of the world. The second part offers readings of work by Kincaid, Long Soldier, and Taha that consider their uses of form and technique in relation to what Wendy Knepper and Sharae Deckard describe as a 'shared history of world-making experiments, [in which dissident texts are] always producing their imaginaries from out of the conditions of struggle' (2016, p. 7). None of the authors addressed in this chapter are as closely connected to organized political movements as those discussed in chapter 5, but, like those author-activists, they engage in forms of literary experiment that seek to imagine a future beyond current conditions of dispossession and inequality, and they encourage their readers to envision that future with them.

Reflection I: Thinking about genre and experiment

1. List at least four examples of literary genres other than the novel. Once you've done this, reflect on (a) what characteristics define each of these genres, meaning how you recognize a genre when you see it; and (b) what literary traditions you associate these genres with. Would you classify them as 'Western' or 'European' genres, for instance? Why or why not?
2. How do you define 'experimental' writing? What kinds of techniques would you expect to see in a work described as experimental? Where does your understanding of this term come from? How does experiment relate to genre?
3. How do you recognize genre and/or experiment in a text that engages with literary traditions that you are not familiar with? What reading strategies or resources might help you with this task?

Genre, tradition, resistance

As I have discussed elsewhere in this book, one of the barriers to decolonizing literary studies is the dominance of a narrow definition of what counts as 'literary' (see Introduction and chapter 1). Postcolonial literary scholars have long wrestled with the idea of the literary, often focusing on the perceived opposition between realist and documentary modes of representation versus non-referential, irreal, and metafictional modes. In classical literary theory, these two orientations are broadly classified as mimesis (imitation of reality) and poiesis (creation of something new). While a number of critics have defended literary realism against the charge of being insufficiently politically or stylistically radical (e.g. Abu-Manneh, 2016; Brennan, 2017; Lazarus, 2011; Sorensen, 2010, 2021), much postcolonial literary scholarship has reinforced the wider tendency in the discipline to equate literary experimentation with the techniques of canonical Western modernism and postmodernism. As John McLeod observes, the 'academic institutionalization' of modernist experimentation as 'characteristically "postcolonial"' has been to the critical detriment of the work of postcolonial writers whose engagement with conventional forms has often been more reverent than contentious, more subtle than dramatic' (2013, p. 450). Like the focus on the novel, the privileging of certain kinds of literary experiment leaves out more literature than it includes. It also overlooks many of the explicitly committed and movement-oriented works that have been central to decolonization struggles, as discussed in chapter 5.

Walter Goebel and Saskia Schabio, in a direct reflection on the question of genre, similarly criticize postcolonial literary studies for its enduring preoccupation with modernist and postmodernist techniques such as subversion and parody. However, they go further than McLeod in seeing this emphasis as a sign of metropolitan readers' ignorance of aesthetic traditions beyond the Euro–US canon. They argue for the need to 'decentre Western aesthetics' by recognizing

Decolonizing Genre 131

the Eurocentrism of dominant literary-critical concepts and terminology; attending to writers' use of pre-colonial 'forms of orature, myth, tale, and communal storytelling'; and developing 'a quasi-anthropological familiarity' with the cultures and languages that inform a given text, in order to avoid 'the imperialist projection of assimilative comparative literature agendas' that simply apply metropolitan formal and stylistic expectations to any text regardless of its origins (Goebel and Schabio, 2012, pp. 1–3). For them, 'aesthetic decolonization' (ibid., p. 3) requires readers and critics to develop critical vocabularies that are informed by a deep knowledge of at least one non-European literary tradition, a claim that echoes Gayatri Chakravorty Spivak's call for an expanded field of comparative literature able to address all literatures with 'linguistic rigor and historical savvy' (2003, p. 13; see also chapter 3).

Goebel and Schabio offer an important challenge to a comparative literary criticism that assumes 'large, widely-recognised, western written genres' (Barber, 2007, p. 41) as a default starting point for interpretation. Yet this argument potentially sits uneasily with my insistence in this book that the decolonization of literary studies requires students and scholars to read as widely as possible. If a reader's effort to engage with a particular text is compromised because they have not (yet) studied the literary tradition(s) from which it emerges, would it be better for them not to read it at all? To be fair, that is not really what Goebel and Schabio are saying. Their point is that the reader must remain conscious of their 'partial insight' and understand that the interpretive challenges presented by a given text are likely to reflect their own lack of knowledge, not the text's 'cultural alterity [difference]' (2012, p. 3). A lack of knowledge can be addressed through wider reading and study; the idea of cultural difference, on the other hand, risks pessimistically assuming that the distance between a reader from one context and a text from another is insurmountable.

This chapter approaches this challenge to the authority of the reader trained in the Western canon as a problem or tension in the decolonization of literary studies, not as

132 Decolonizing Genre

an absolute limit. It is important to reiterate, however, that such a significant deficit in background knowledge is not something that can be easily or quickly resolved by the diversification of the literature curriculum. It demands that we study not only diverse literary traditions but also diverse *critical* traditions, since, as Karin Barber points out, 'genres are often set up hand-in-glove with explicit, elaborated genres of exegesis and interpretation ... [T]he means to interpret them ... are themselves a tradition, and one that can be just as revealing as the textual tradition itself' (2007, p. 5). To be sure, the task of achieving familiarity with multiple critical traditions is more easily said than done. This is not just because there are so many traditions to study, but also because literary criticism written in languages other than English (and perhaps French) is even less likely to be translated than literary texts. This means that a comprehensive engagement with a non-European critical tradition will often require mastery of the language in which it is written (see also chapter 3). However, a reader can begin by drawing on the guidance of other critics. For instance, there is a growing body of overviews of regional and linguistic literary and critical traditions from around the world that have been published in English; such texts can point the way to further study of a particular period, language, and/or region.[24]

When we consider writers' engagements with genre, the need to read across critical traditions becomes even clearer. Firstly, this focus draws attention once again to the limits of canonical Western genre categories; and, secondly, it challenges the tendency in dominant formations of literary studies to understand generic innovation as a sign of the writer's individual genius (cf. Goebel and Schabio, 2012, p. 3). The writers I address in this chapter are often praised for their creative challenges to genre boundaries and conventions, as I discuss in the next section. Yet the formation and evolution of genres is best understood as a collective endeavour: genres emerge from a particular place and time, they develop in response to the changing influences of popular and communal forms, and their parameters depend on the writer and reader's familiarity with 'a host of conventions

Decolonizing Genre

and expectations' associated with that genre (Barber, 2007, p. 34). In other words, genres cannot be interpreted in isolation from their historical and social contexts. The public and collective dimension of genre is often especially visible in forms such as drama and spoken word poetry, where the centrality of performance foregrounds the audience's expectations. However, it can also be seen in print forms such as the short story collection, which has a genealogical relationship to the story cycles of oral narrative. Therefore, rather than understanding genre primarily in relation to the individual artist's disruption or transgression of genre conventions – as emphasized by the 'modernist literary dominant' (Brennan, 2017, p. 267; see also chapters 1 and 5) – we might instead prioritize the repetition and reproduction of tradition that Barber identifies as key to texts' participation in a genre. All texts 'renew [the] generic field in the act of drawing from it; all, in some sense, feed back into it and become material or models on which other, new productions draw' (Barber, 2007, p. 25).

In any case, when addressing literary production in formerly colonized contexts, individual artists cannot be understood as the only source of disruption of tradition. As I have noted in previous chapters, the imposition of European colonial languages and education systems on colonized regions had an enormous impact on their literary and cultural production, one that few if any pre-colonial genres managed to escape. Genre has thus been a particularly important site for anticolonial and postcolonial writers' appropriation and contestation of colonial cultural legacies, as seen in my discussion of the practice of 'writing back' in chapter 4. Peter Hitchcock goes so far as to argue that the 'instability of genre' in postcolonial writing should be seen as 'part of the texture of decolonization itself, where generic extension explodes all orderly transfers of power' (2017, p. 168; see also Hitchcock, 2003). Hitchcock's point is that genre becomes part of the terrain of struggle in the process of decolonization, not least because some genres become closely associated with aspects of colonial history and others with anticolonial resistance. For example, the novel has often been seen as an 'imported' imperial form in formerly colonized regions, giving rise to long-running debates about whether its development can in fact be traced to pre-colonial narrative forms or whether it is entirely 'foreign'.[25] Meanwhile, poetry (a very capacious genre) has played an enormous role in anticolonial struggles across the globe, as well as in post-independence protests against the postcolonial state, because of poetry's relative ease of production and circulation and its frequent invocation of pre-colonial oral and written textual traditions.[26] In the end, the question of whether a specific genre is appropriated or indigenous is often impossible to resolve, and arguably beside the point. It is how writers affirm, adapt, combine, and shift between conventions that are associated with a genre, in dialogue with other texts and artists and with their audience, that determines that genre's uses and meanings in the present.

This brings us to a more nuanced way of understanding the work of the individual artist. Rather than seeing a writer's deployment or disruption of genre conventions as part of their 'genius', it is more productive to understand their use of genre and other techniques as part of their artistic practice, which draws on the tools, institutions, and networks of relation that are available to them in a particular place and time. Arguing for a renewed attention to craft in postcolonial literary studies, Ben Etherington, Jarad Zimbler, and Rachel Bower offer a more precise understanding of the idea of individual 'innovation' by emphasizing the writer's labour and agency, meaning the ways in which the writer's decisions produce the effects of their works (2014, p. 275). In a subsequent essay, Etherington and Zimbler further argue that the use of technique should be seen as intimately connected to the writer's political project: 'To ensure the truth strikes home with sudden immediacy, the novelist will need to do something other than re-present to readers well-handled items from the trove of gathered images; something other still than seizing or even shattering those images' (2014, p. 281; see also Etherington and Zimbler, 2021). This final point suggests that, instead of celebrating generic and other forms of disruption for their own sake, we should pay attention

Decolonizing Genre

to writers who can be seen as actively reworking the shared practices of the literary field(s) in which they participate. The parameters of their field(s) include language; place and time; and the writer's use of form and technique, which will necessarily require choices about genre. In the discussion that follows, I suggest some of the ways we might see this active engagement with the constraints and possibilities of genre in the service of an anticolonial political and intellectual project in the work of Kincaid, Long Soldier, and Taha.

Summary

- Scholarship in metropolitan postcolonial studies has often reinforced ideas of the 'literary' and the 'experimental' that are drawn from the Western literary and critical canon, particularly from Euro–US traditions of modernism and postmodernism. This emphasis has excluded many other literary traditions.
- The decolonization of literary studies requires readers to familiarize themselves with aesthetic traditions beyond the Western canon. This effort requires more than the diversification of our reading lists; it means drawing on the guidance of critics with regional expertise and studying the languages of non-European critical traditions.
- Genre emphasizes the need to study different traditions because it calls attention to the historical and social dimensions of literary production. Instead of focusing only on an individual artist's disruption of genre conventions, we might also consider their participation in the reproduction and continuation of genres.
- Genre is also a key means of contesting colonial cultural legacies. Genres carry associations with different aspects of pre-colonial, colonial, and anticolonial culture that inform readers' expectations. Writers can affirm, interrogate, or play with

> such expectations as part of their artistic practice, further contributing to the development of genres.
>
> - Genre can be understood as one of the many tools available to writers in the literary field(s) in which they work. Writers make active decisions about how to deploy such tools, which means that their use of form and technique is closely intertwined with their intellectual and political projects.

'Language disassembled into glittering shards': genre, experiment, and anticolonial critique

The writers considered in this section belong to different generations, but they share an identity as women, a straddling of 'Western' and 'non-Western' geographical and institutional locations, and an enthusiastic reception as literary innovators. Jamaica Kincaid, who is originally from Antigua but long resident in the United States, has been awarded numerous literary prizes over her forty-year career, including a Guggenheim award, the Prix Femina étranger, and memberships in the American Academies of Arts and Letters and Arts and Sciences. Layli Long Soldier, an Oglala Lakota (Indigenous American) poet from the US Southwest, has won and been nominated for several North American prizes, including a National Book Critics Circle award and a PEN/Jean Stein award. Dalia Taha, a Palestinian playwright and poet from Ramallah who writes primarily in Arabic but whose work has been translated into English and other European languages, has a longstanding relationship with the Royal Court Theatre in London and has had work produced in the US, Belgium, and Germany as well as Palestine and Morocco.

Kincaid's short story collection *At the Bottom of the River* (1983), Long Soldier's poetry collection *Whereas* (2017), and Taha's plays *Keffiyeh/Made in China* (2012) and *Fireworks* (2015) all draw on recognizably modernist forms of literary experiment, including fragmentation, contradiction, and juxtaposition of different voices, narrative styles, and visual layouts. In contrast to the texts discussed in chapter 5 and indeed much of the rest of this book, they tend to eschew direct argument and more openly refuse the assumption that they will represent the experiences of people who share the author's background. Taha, in a newspaper interview conducted during rehearsals for *Fireworks* at the Royal Court, makes this stance explicit: 'People, especially in the west, have specific expectations. You expect us to make a political statement, to tell the story of our suffering. ... [Art is] always responding to politics. But at the same time it's art, so it's also doing something else. It's playing with aesthetics and form. I'm trying to respond to both' (Moss, 2015).

Importantly, as this final statement suggests, Taha is not simply defending her individual freedom as an artist. Instead, she insists that her work's meditations on race, gender, nation, empire, and resistance cannot be separated from her use of form and technique, as is also the case for Kincaid and Long Soldier. This interdependence of form and content can be seen in the description of Long Soldier's work I have cited in the title of this section, which is taken from a *Los Angeles Times* review of *Whereas*: 'You do not slip into this book on silken bolts of easy beauty, but scratch yourself raw on language disassembled into glittering shards' (Freeman, 2017). Taha's *Keffiyeh/Made in China* has been described using the same metaphor in reference to her use of disconnected scenes: 'The play as a whole sat as *a series of shards*; fragments reminiscent of the Palestinian land and, perhaps, its sense of self today' (Mohammad, 2014, p. 29; emphasis added). The image of the shard posits language (in Long Soldier's case) and form (in Taha's) as weapons of struggle. It imagines their craft as capable of causing damage, to an enemy or an idea or the reader themselves. This confrontational quality is also strongly associated with Kincaid's work, above all her anti-imperial and anti-capitalist polemic *A Small Place* (1988), which links the legacies of colonial rule and slavery to the contemporary tourist industry in Antigua. Although *A Small Place* is Kincaid's most critically influential

138   Decolonizing Genre

work, it was reportedly rejected for publication in the *New Yorker* magazine (her then employer) because the editor found it 'too angry and bitter'; the book and its author were also banned for a time in Antigua (Hansen, 2016, p. 32). *At the Bottom of the River* is less openly adversarial in its tone and subject matter but equally condemning of the forces of imperial, institutional, and patriarchal violence that underpin each story.

These writers' anticolonial politics can also be seen in their direct and indirect evocations of the devastation wreaked on Caribbean, Indigenous American, and Palestinian people and landscapes and in their efforts to make historical and ongoing liberation struggles visible. As the *Los Angeles Times* review says of Long Soldier: 'she practices the crime scene forensics and ancestor respect of a poet used to growing up on the erased people's ledger of American empire' (Freeman, 2017). This idea of combining 'crime scene forensics' with 'ancestor respect' is a useful way of thinking about the uses of genre by Long Soldier and the other writers. It points not only to their interweaving of mimetic and poetic modes of representation but also to their awareness of the relationship of their work to broader regional traditions. Taha dedicates *Keffiyeh/Made in China* to the Palestinian theatre directors Julian Mer Khamis and François Abu Salem (2015b [2012], p. 71); Kincaid invokes the West African and creole river goddess Mammywata (cf. Cobham, 2002); and Long Soldier incorporates Lakota words into her English-language text and refuses stereotypical representations of Indigenous cultural practice: '*Beware, a horse isn't a reference to my heritage*' (2019 [2017], p. 74). Their work can thus be seen as reparative as well as accusatory, since each text foregrounds literature's capacity to affirm an obscured past and envision a more emancipatory future. Finally, an anticolonial politics arises from each writer's invitation to the reader to participate actively in the experience of reading the text. Long Soldier leaves out words, inviting the reader to 'co-author the text by filling in the blanks' (Hoover, 2017, p. E11); Taha makes the reader work to connect decontextualized dialogues to their geographical and historical settings; and Kincaid's fluid

Decolonizing Genre

movement between unnamed narrators and settings asks the reader to reconstruct the links between her characters' circumstances and their experiences, revealing the latter 'to be the creation of concrete historical processes whose continuing manifestations can be battled in the here and now' (Alessandrini, 2010, p. 563).

Kincaid's *At the Bottom of the River* demonstrates the versatility of the short story as a genre, since the only defining feature of this form is its shortness. The ten stories in the collection have been described as 'prose poems' (Nasta, 2009, p. 70; Rabea and Almahameed, 2018, p. 158) because of their precise use of imagery and of a stylized first-person narrator, who usually seems to be a version of the author as a girl or young woman. Clues to the speaker's age and gender appear here and there: she makes statements such as 'Now I am a girl' and 'I shall grow up to be a woman', although at other times her mother's voice takes over: 'I see my child arise slowly from her bed' (Kincaid, 1985 [1983], pp. 11, 22, 49). The stories also draw on the genres of life writing and the *Bildungsroman* (coming-of-age narrative) by apparently tracing the trajectory of the protagonist's development over the course of the collection, and on the family saga or domestic drama by centring the protagonist's relationship with her mother. Most of the stories also seem to be set in the Caribbean. Evidence of the location emerges in Kincaid's use of Caribbean English speech patterns in some passages of monologue and dialogue and in her references to plants, animals, foods, landscape, and African-Caribbean folk cultures and belief systems. For instance, the narrator's mother warns her against the 'jablesse' (La Diablesse, a malevolent spirit who takes the form of a beautiful woman), and later the mother herself takes the form of a lizard (Kincaid, 1985, pp. 8–9, 55). However, because the reader must continually work to determine who is speaking and what they are speaking about, the stories resist the expectation that they will provide ready information about the author/narrator and her location.

Moreover, only the first story, 'Girl', a monologue delivered by a mother instructing and criticizing her daughter, remains

140 Decolonizing Genre

wholly in the realm of the real. The rest of the stories are increasingly taken over by irreal characters and events, from the dead man who stands outside the house where he used to live, to the speaker's encompassing vision of the whole world reproduced anew and undivided 'at the bottom of the river' in the final titular story (Kincaid, 1985, pp. 7–8, 77–8). The encroachment of the irreal makes the stories increasingly disorienting, particularly for a reader who is not familiar with the belief systems being invoked.[27] While the stories' irreal elements are generally presented as sinister or threatening, in the final story the narrator reclaims them as a source of strength. She enters the sea and finds

> [h]ow good this water was. How good that I should know no fear. ... I had no name for the thing I had become, so new was it to me, except that I did not exist in pain or pleasure, east or west or north or south, or up or down, or past or present or future, or real or not real. ... [H]ow bound up I know I am to all that is human endeavor, to all that is past and to all that shall be, to all that shall be lost and leave no trace. I claim these things then – mine – and now feel myself grow solid and complete, my name filling up my mouth. (Ibid., pp. 79–82)

The collection ends on this note of triumphant self-knowledge, grounded in the awareness of the speaker's connection to a past and future that encompasses human agency and creation, non-human life and the environment, and the spiritual and ancestral world.

In its title, and especially in this final story, the collection draws on the figure of the West African female water spirit Mammywata, known in Jamaica and elsewhere in the Caribbean as 'River Mumma' (Cobham, 2002, p. 871). In 'At the bottom of the river', a woman who resembles this spirit leads the narrator to her vision of a new world:

> Her skin was the color of brown clay, and she looked like a statue, liquid and gleaming, just before it is to be

Decolonizing Genre 141

put in a kiln. ... [S]he looked at something that was far,
far away from where she stood. I got down on my knees
and I looked, too. It was a long time before I could see
what it was that she saw. (Kincaid, 1985, pp. 76–7)

As Rhonda Cobham has observed, the Mammywata also
appears in Kincaid's later novel *The Autobiography of My
Mother* (1997), where she symbolizes a suppressed African-
Caribbean cultural heritage 'that everyone recognizes, though
no one will valorize' (2002, p. 875). Cobham contends that
Kincaid refuses the relegation of 'African derived systems
of belief and knowledge' to the subconscious that so often
occurs in Caribbean literature and culture, instead making
them central to her characters' quests to refashion themselves
and the world around them (ibid., pp. 874, 880–1).

This revalorization of African-Caribbean tradition is
closely related to Kincaid's decisions about genre, again
foregrounding the interdependence of form and content
in her work. Her use of the short-story cycle invokes the
practice of oral storytelling, which the Barbadian poet and
critic Kamau Brathwaite has famously identified as central
to Caribbean language and literature: 'the noise and sounds
that the poet makes are responded to by the audience and
are returned to him' (1993, p. 273; see also chapter 3). The
form of the short-story collection also promotes a continuity
of themes and motifs that can be revisited and reworked in
subsequent stories, recalling the speaker's self-description
in 'At the bottom of the river' as 'if I were a prism, many-
sided and transparent, refracting and reflecting light as it
reached me, light that could never be destroyed' (Kincaid,
1985, p. 80). This conceit evokes Kincaid's own practice of
returning to certain characters, events, and settings again and
again, both within this collection and across her entire body
of work (Nasta, 2009, pp. 65, 72). It also resonates with
local artistic practices that 'reflect' pre-colonial cultural and
narrative traditions but also 'refract' them as part of ongoing
struggles against empire, slavery, and their legacies that
continue after formal independence. Kincaid incorporates the
reference points and worldviews of these collective struggles

into her own practice of anticolonial critique, reframing and reimagining them as she goes.

In Layli Long Soldier's poetry, form and subject matter are similarly interdependent. Long Soldier cites the idea of craft as key to her writing practice: 'Craft is a way, too. We need tools. We need things. Language is immaterial, but it's through certain devices or tools that we have in working with the language that I think, magically or miraculously, help me access that place as well' (Stosuy, 2021). *Whereas*, her first book-length collection, is made up of two parts. Part I is a series of shorter lyric poems concerned with the speaker's experiences as a member of the Oglala Lakota Nation, a poet, and a mother. Part II consists of one long poem, 'Whereas', which responds critically to the United States Congress's formal apology to Indigenous Americans (S.J.Res. 14, 2009). The collection begins and ends with the phrase 'grassesgrassesgrasses', which refers both to the Lakotas' ancestral grassland territories and (as Long Soldier explains) to Dakota[28] fighters' revenge killing of a white storekeeper in 1862. The man had justified his refusal of credit to starving Dakota people by saying, 'If they are hungry, let them eat grass'; when his body was found, 'his mouth was stuffed with grass' (Long Soldier, 2019, p. 53). The phrase thus signals Long Soldier's effort to construct within her poems a 'resistant, reparative space' (Falci, 2020, p. 85) that draws on Indigenous practices of land stewardship and histories of collective struggle and survival.

The collection makes use of techniques that are already associated with 'experimental' poetry in the contemporary anglophone literary landscape, including the use of different page layouts and the poet's frequent meta-commentary on her choice of words and images. However, in each instance Long Soldier makes it clear that this experimentation is closely tied to the political intentions of her work. For example, the opening poem is titled 'Ȟe Sápa', which is the Lakota name for a mountain range in present-day South Dakota, known in English by the translation 'Black Hills'. The territory was promised to the Lakota in an 1868 treaty that was almost immediately broken when gold was discovered there in

Decolonizing Genre 143

1874; the Lakota were then violently expelled. Long Soldier does not summarize this history – the reader must look it up for themselves – but each of the poem's five sections allude to this dispossession. The third section of the poem does so visually: its four lines are arranged in a square, evoking the fenced-off space of the reservations where displaced Lakota and other Indigenous Americans were forced to live after their land had been seized (Long Soldier, 2019, p. 8). Another experiment with layout, which Long Soldier calls a 'marginal / slope corner arrange / ment' because of her use of right-justified stanzas containing lines of increasing length (ibid., p. 17), appears in the poem 'Diction'. Here she cites a popular history of the US Army massacre of Lakota people at Wounded Knee in 1890, written by the Blackfeet/A'ainin novelist James Welch (Welch, 1994; see Long Soldier, 2019). But, again, a reader looking for a historical account of the massacre will be disappointed, since half the words from the original text are missing: 'By way of contrast, / were still coming. By / Knee, the population of / 0, there would be only / reservations in the west' (Long Soldier, 2019, p. 17). Long Soldier's redactions invite the reader to search out the missing information while also registering the magnitude of the Lakotas' loss in the cryptic phrases that remain. By contrast, other poems provide the reader with plenty of information and do not ask them to fill in the gaps. '38', which tells the story of the mass execution of thirty-eight Dakota men by Abraham Lincoln's administration after their armed uprising, is narrated in prose arranged in long lines of poetry. Long Soldier affirms that this choice of layout and syntax is part of a documentary representation: 'Here, the sentence will be respected. ... I do not regard this as a poem of great imagination or a work of fiction' (ibid., p. 49).

Long Soldier's meditations on language and word choice often address her position as an Oglala Lakota poet who can write only in English, recalling the concerns of the anglophone Caribbean poets discussed in chapter 3. She incorporates Lakota words, often as titles of poems, and reflects on their meanings, but she also feels ashamed of her lack of mastery of the language: 'I beg from a dictionary

144 Decolonizing Genre

to learn our word for *poor* comma in a language I dare to call *my* language comma who am I' (Long Soldier, 2019, p. 44). By contrast, when she considers English words, she often emphasizes the use of language to cover up acts of violence. In '38', she 'translates' into plain speech the opaque language of US law that sanctioned the Dakotas' dispossession: 'As treaties were abrogated (broken)'; 'the northern portion was ceded (taken)'; 'living within assigned boundaries (a reservation)' (ibid., pp. 50–1). She describes the result of these legal procedures in even blunter language – 'The Dakota people starved' – and advises the reader to read this last line 'as a straightforward and plainly stated fact' (ibid., p. 51).

These approaches to layout and language continue in the long poem 'Whereas', which is the centrepiece of the collection and has received the most critical attention. The poem takes S.J.Res. 14 (111th Congress), an official apology to Indigenous Americans that was signed by President Barack Obama in 2009, as a formal and political point of departure. The government apology to Indigenous peoples is part of a 'relatively recent genre of political writing in the West', with other settler-colonial states including Canada, Norway, Sweden, and Australia having issued similar statements (Griffis, 2020, p. 53). The US version is notable not only for its rather feeble language of apology – it mitigates its admission of US settler violence by affirming the settlers' 'desire for a just relationship with the Indian tribes' and lamenting the loss of life on 'both' sides (US Congress, 2009) – but also because Obama never read it aloud, and its sponsor Senator Sam Brownback later read it to only five tribal leaders (Long Soldier, 2019, p. 57). The apology itself was an addendum to a military appropriations bill, making it 'a deeply problematic speech act: a non-apology apology buried within a weapons bill that ensures further "depredations" on a massive scale in other parts of the world' (Falci, 2020, p. 79).

In Long Soldier's poetic response, the congressional apology's use of the word 'whereas' (which begins a list of twenty statements) becomes an 'anaphoric catalyst for

Decolonizing Genre

an investigative account' (Falci, 2020, p. 78). Long Soldier offers her own series of anaphoric statements beginning with 'whereas' as counterpoint and challenge to the original text: 'Whereas when offered an apology I watch each movement the shoulders / high or folding'; 'Whereas at four years old I read the first chapter of the Bible aloud I was not Christian'; 'Whereas I read an article in the *New York Times* about the federal sequestration of funds from reservation programs, the cuts' (2019, pp. 61, 63, 84). Continuing her attention to the violence that language can conceal, she challenges the presumptiveness of the word 'whereas' itself, which assigns all power to the speaker and not the addressee: 'Whereas sets the table. The cloth. The saltshakers and plates. Whereas calls me to the table. Whereas precedes and invites' (ibid., p. 79).

In keeping with the format of the original document, Long Soldier follows her series of 'whereas' statements with a list of 'resolutions'. In this section she returns to experiments with layout, deconstructing the apology's promises in order to expose their meaninglessness and hypocrisy. For example, she blacks out the word 'apologizes' from the main statement of apology, on the grounds that there is no word for 'apologize' in many Indigenous American languages, thereby emphasizing the apology's lack of substance. She rearranges the text of another passage in the form of a hammer to '*reveal in a text the shape of its pounding*' (2019, pp. 92–3). She then counters the document's empty resolutions with a resolution of her own, inspired by the 2016–17 protests against the Dakota Access Pipeline at the Standing Rock reservation:

we are Protectors
we are peaceful & prayerful
here we all stand together
we are non-violent
we are proud to stand
no masks
respect locals
no weapons (Ibid., p. 95)

146   Decolonizing Genre

In this section of the poem, Long Soldier makes it clear that language – even the English language – is not only a tool of oppression. It is also possible to forge 'responsible ways of speaking and writing' (Griffis, 2020, p. 67), which in this passage are derived from a collective movement of resistance to the further destruction of the land and livelihoods of Lakota and Dakota peoples. Long Soldier offers poetry as a form that 'grounds words in truth, reality, and fidelity to material phenomena' (ibid., p. 70) and affirms her commitment as a poet to refute the falsehoods of US colonial history and help imagine a liberatory future.

Like Long Soldier, the Palestinian playwright Dalia Taha wrestles with the practical and political implications of narrating her national community's history and experiences to an outside audience. She shares this concern with many other contemporary Palestinian artists, who are often either located outside of historic Palestine or working in Palestine/Israel with external sponsorship (this is particularly true for theatre practitioners and filmmakers, who need substantial funding). As Rania Jawad has observed, for Palestinians, 'the need to write, study, and document themselves has been intricately entwined with the struggle for national self-representation and self-determination.' Yet this demand compels Palestinians to constantly perform their status as human beings for metropolitan spectators who 'evaluat[e] and judg[e] this performance'. This effort problematically substitutes the politics of recognition for anticolonial struggle: 'to be recognized as human does not equal liberation' (Jawad, 2014, pp. 35–7).

Taha's resistance to the demand to 'tell the story of our suffering' (Moss, 2015) signals her refusal to perform Palestinian humanity according to this script. Her work has mainly been staged outside of Palestine with funding from international sponsors, above all the Royal Court Theatre, which has a long history of supporting Palestinian and other Arab playwrights and staging plays about Palestine (Mohammad, 2014, p. 28; Bernard, 2014, p. 166). This does not mean that her plays are directed only at non-Palestinian audiences; *Keffiyeh/Made in China* toured seven Palestinian

West Bank cities after its premiere in Brussels (Taha, 2015b, p. 126), and in any case metropolitan audiences also include members of the Palestinian diaspora. Nevertheless, Taha's experiments with theatrical form can be understood as a reaction to what Richard Twyman, the director of the Royal Court production of *Fireworks*, calls the 'calcification of imagery from Palestine', particularly in international media, since her settings, staging, and characters tend to be 'incongruous with an expectation of what Palestine is' (Taha and Twyman, 2015). Her plays rely heavily on techniques of defamiliarization and estrangement, including unspecified settings, non-linear plotting, and an emphasis on the fragmentation or disintegration of language (ibid.). Taha writes in the author's statement at the start of the published English-language script of *Keffiyeh/Made in China* that, '[o]f all the art forms, [theatre] is the one that relies most on what is avoided ... I believe in theater because it doesn't make us happy' (2015b, p. 69). She thus identifies theatre as especially suited to resisting the audience's desire for information, as well as the kind of feel-good ending that can allow a viewer to feel that their political duties have been fulfilled by simply watching a play.

Taha's effort to challenge audience expectations about Palestine is evident in *Keffiyeh/Made in China*, which consists of ten self-contained vignettes, all but one of which take the form of a dialogue between two unidentified characters. Some scenes hint at a Palestinian setting: 'Craving mangoes' mentions children throwing stones, 'Crowdedness' takes place in the queue for a checkpoint, and 'The prisoner and the other prisoner' is set in a prison cell. But these aspects of Palestinian life are subordinated to petty domestic disputes between family members or obscured by fractured dialogues that the viewer must work to follow. The vignette 'Business' falls in the latter category, staging an increasingly disjointed dialogue between a shopkeeper (M, for 'man') and a young Belgian woman (G, for 'girl') who wants to buy a keffiyeh, the black-and-white patterned headscarf that has become an international icon of Palestinian resistance (the play's title comes from this scene). Yet this fragmentation of language is not merely an aesthetic choice, for Taha makes it clear that the characters' inability to communicate results from G's entrenched ignorance. When M tries to sell her a blue bra instead of a keffiyeh, in reference to a widely circulated video of Egyptian soldiers dragging the half-clothed body of an unconscious female protestor in Cairo's Tahrir Square in December 2011, G assumes that he is sexually harassing her. Taha gives the viewer who may not recognize the reference to the Tahrir protests more context:

> M: I think you haven't seen the video yet.
> G: Aren't you ashamed?
> M: The Egyptian girl dragged along by the soldiers.
> G: What Egyptian girl?
> M: The images are famous throughout the world.
> G: I've never been to Egypt.
> M: Don't you follow the news?
> G: I don't do politics. (Taha, 2015b, p. 99)

G's responses to M are not quite non-sequiturs, but they consistently fail to engage with what he has said, highlighting her arrogance and lack of curiosity about the exchange. She wants the keffiyeh as a fashionable symbol of Palestine solidarity, but she does not want to hear from Palestinians themselves. Taha illustrates this dynamic through the construction of the scene as well as its content, with each pair of lines highlighting a missed opportunity for G to listen to what M has to say, thus emphasizing the limits of a humanitarian politics of recognition.

In addition to challenging the clichés of international perception of Palestinians, Taha's plays offer more empowering representations. As she says in her author's statement, she writes about 'ordinary people in extraordinary circumstances', arguing that 'it's only theater that could establish the threat of collapse as a collective experience: understanding the consequences and the stakes of such moments, and our responsibilities as humans and individuals in relation to them' (Taha, 2015b, p. 69). Her inclusion in *Keffiyeh/Made in China* of multiple scenes of couples arguing

Decolonizing Genre

over domestic chores in the midst of repression and atrocity – the glimpse of an old woman queuing for hours at a checkpoint ('Crowdedness'), the release of a father from prison ('The green glasses'), the death of a child ('Craving mangoes', 'Redecoration') – emphasizes the horrifying normality of such violence as something that affects all Palestinians living under occupation. In *Fireworks*, she develops this idea further by focusing on two Palestinian families living in the same apartment block during what appears to be the 2014 Israeli invasion of Gaza, which took place while she was working on the play (Taha and Twyman, 2015). This play is less formally discontinuous than *Keffiyeh/Made in China*: the scenes are broadly sequential and the named characters remain constant over the course of the play. Two of the protagonists are children, in a possible comment on the reliance on children's testimony in humanitarian Palestine advocacy (cf. Jawad, 2014, p. 33); the others are their parents, who are mired in their own grief and fear but still desperately concerned with keeping their children safe.

This dynamic reaches a climax in a monologue delivered by one of the fathers, Khalid, about his grief at the loss of his teenage son Ali, who was shot by an Israeli soldier six months earlier. Until now, the focus has been on the boy's mother's anguish, but here Khalid expresses his own:

> I have to pretend that I'm not lying on the floor and watching the sky. I have to pretend that the screams I'm hearing come from the TV. I have to pretend that his grave is as small as a pebble. I have to pretend they didn't put his body in a plastic bag. I have to pretend to watch them collecting the bits of his body on the TV. I have to pretend that the children who are running are chasing a clown. I have to sew up his wounds with my bare hands. I forgot my baby boy's name. (Taha, 2015a, p. 74)

This moment could be read as fulfilling the demand that Palestinians perform their humanity. However, by setting Khalid's excruciating grief against the backdrop of the ongoing

150   Decolonizing Genre

bombing of Gaza, Taha makes the point that his loss is part of a shared and ongoing destruction of people's bodies and lives. It is equally important that Khalid is not alone on stage at this moment. The stage directions indicate that he grabs a pistol and tries to shoot himself, but can't. The other father, Ahmad, who has been on stage listening to this monologue, hugs him, and '[t]he two men cry' (ibid.). Here Taha emphasizes the idea of 'the threat of collapse as a collective experience' (2015b, p. 69). Khalid and Ahmad are connected not only by their shared grief (shortly afterwards, in the play's final scene, Ahmad will lose his own son to an 'explosion', presumably a missile strike) but by their recognition of the collective nature of their suffering. Taha thus shares with Kincaid and Long Soldier an insistence on locating their protagonists' experiences within a shared past and present, and, like them, she draws on the tools of her craft to gesture towards the possibility of a different kind of common future.

Reflection II: Genre and decolonization

1. To what extent can Kincaid, Long Solider, and Taha be classified as working 'within' Western canonical genres and aesthetic traditions? How do they extend or challenge the conventions of their genres? How do their engagements with other aesthetic traditions contribute to this task?

2. What do you make of the idea that language and form can be seen as weapons in the struggle for decolonization? Do you think this is a valid characterization of the work of Kincaid, Long Solider, and Taha? Can you name any other texts whose aesthetic techniques might be described in this way?

3. What are some of the specific generic properties of the short story, poetry, and drama that might help support decolonization struggles? Feel free to draw in your response on the discussion in this chapter or on other texts you know.

Conclusion

As much as has been achieved we are only at the beginning of a very long struggle. The challenge now is to continue onto the next battles and win the war for knowledge that leads to liberation and overturning the colonial status quo.

Kehinde Andrews (2018)

As I was completing this book in early 2022, global headlines were consumed with the Russian invasion of Ukraine and the flight of millions of Ukrainian refugees to other countries in Europe. The Russian invasion was blatantly imperial in its vision: it sought to bring Ukraine under Russian control against the wishes of most of its inhabitants and employed the full force of the Russian military to do so. Many European countries swiftly opened their borders to the Ukrainian refugees and gave them accommodation and material support. Yet this inspiring show of solidarity was tempered by the stark contrast with the treatment of refugees from other countries at the same border sites by the same governments. For example, Iraqi and Afghan refugees had been violently denied entry to Poland only a few months earlier (Kennedy and Mortensen, 2021), and the informal encampments at Calais, France, housed many refugees from West and Central Asia and sub-Saharan Africa trying to make their way to the UK with virtually no legal way of doing so, even though these migrants' journeys had often been precipitated by wars waged by the UK, the US, and their allies

(Sajjad, 2022; Sanderson, 2022). Governments across the world also quickly imposed an economic boycott and international sanctions on Russia, very much along the lines of what Palestinians and Palestine solidarity activists have been demanding be placed on Israel for decades (Marcetic, 2022). The markedly different response to the Ukrainian crisis made it difficult to conclude that anything other than racism was at work. Indeed, across mainstream metropolitan media, the language used to describe the Ukrainian refugees often openly privileged their status as white Christian Europeans who were more deserving of asylum than Black, Brown, and/or Muslim migrants from former European colonies (Euro-Med Human Rights Monitor, 2022).

I end with this example to reiterate a key premise of this book, namely that contemporary crises such as mass forced migration, statelessness, and climate collapse cannot be separated from the structural racism and violence that characterize the imperial past and present. When the capital of the Quinault nation, an Indigenous American tribe based on a reservation in Washington state, is urgently threatened by rising sea levels but the residents have no way of moving their town uphill (Ufberg, 2022), or when Israeli police destroy Palestinian homes and businesses in the Sheikh Jarrah neighbourhood in East Jerusalem to make room for more Jewish Israeli settlement (Nassar, 2022), these events must be understood as part of the long and ongoing history of settler-colonial seizures of land and resources in these sites. They are also part of the continuing struggles to resist such oppression. These injustices would not make the news at all were it not for local activists' efforts to stand up to this violence, be it spectacular – as in the Israeli demolitions of Palestinian homes – or slow (Nixon, 2011), as in the latest displacement of the Quinault people.

We may understandably feel cynical about what journalism, let alone other literary forms, can achieve in the face of this level of destruction. How many bystanders read these reports in the mainstream media, much less the activist press? How many of those who do read about these events will act in response to what they have read? Does signing a petition or

Conclusion 153

attending a demonstration count as having acted? Do such actions make a difference, any more than reading a poem or a novel does? Certainly, part of my argument in this book is that reading by itself is not enough. It is not enough to read an account of someone else's dispossession while sitting safely in one's own home. It is not enough to discuss a text in a university classroom, a space from which so many people continue to be excluded. However, I have also been trying to make the case that reading still matters. Our political responsibilities are not discharged by the act of reading, but they are awakened, illuminated, explored, tested, and expanded. The daily barrage of news headlines, especially from locations that are geographically distant to one's own, might feel grimly disempowering. But one of the things that I have sought to show is the range of ways in which literary texts can resist that kind of disillusionment and detachment. Literary texts do not only reflect what is. They ask their readers to recognize our assumptions about how the world around us works and how we got here, and to approach what we think we know with fresh eyes. By making it possible to see the past and present differently, they invite us to contemplate a different collective future.

This book has explored some of the ways that literary texts carry out this work, drawing attention to their use of language, form, and style as well as content. It has been especially concerned with how we as readers and critics can recognize and respond to the political work that texts do, with particular attention to the responsibilities of those of us who are based in metropolitan anglophone universities. I have maintained throughout the book that how we read matters as much as what we read and that, while dominant formations of literary studies have come a long way on both fronts in the last several decades, there is still a long way to go before our discipline can claim to be 'overturning the colonial status quo', as Kehinde Andrews puts it in the epigraph to this chapter. We need more geographical and linguistic range, not only in our readings of modern and contemporary literature – which has been my focus in this book – but also in our readings of older texts.[29] We need more engagement

154 Conclusion

with critical traditions from beyond Western Europe and North America and with literary traditions that are not written down. We need more creative and rigorous strategies for comparing texts from different places, times, and standpoints. We need more interaction between reading and writing that takes place in formal educational settings and that which takes place outside them. We need more recognition and respect for modes of writing that are not routinely classed as 'literary' and more critical strategies and sharing of knowledge to enable readers to engage with such texts. We need more translation, publishing, and distribution of literary texts and criticism written in non-metropolitan languages, more open access to scholarship, and more opportunities for scholars based in universities in the Global South to get their work widely read and discussed.

I have tried to strike a balance between, on the one hand, being alert to the ways in which the work of decolonizing literature might be compromised or constrained for students and scholars who benefit from institutional, racial, economic, and other kinds of privilege; and, on the other hand, insisting that this is work that everyone must do from their respective standpoints. I have also tried to stress that decolonizing literature is an ongoing, open-ended process, and that it is necessarily collaborative, involving writers, readers, students, teachers, activists, and critics from a wide range of backgrounds and locations. Part of our task as readers is to think about who we are in conversation with, both on the page (meaning what we read) and also in our wider communities: that is, who we read alongside.

Literary criticism has its own important role to play in the continuing work of decolonizing the discipline, because it offers a space for sustained and informed contemplation of reading, writing, and listening and the relationship of these activities to movements for political, social, and economic justice. By literary criticism, I mean any work that strives for reflective and knowledgeable engagement with literary texts: this includes published scholarship but also classroom essays, contributions to online journals and literary magazines, and so on. There is a growing body of criticism that is

Conclusion 155

explicitly concerned with the questions I have raised in this book. This criticism explores different ways of addressing the political work of literature, bolstered by an inclusive understanding of what literature is, and it strives to view literature and the world from a vantage point other than that of the metropolitan centres. It includes scholarship on literature's relationship to local and international activist movements (e.g. Gopal, 2019; O. Harrison, 2015, 2023; Majumder, 2020; Saha, 2019); environmental collapse (e.g. Deckard, 2020, 2021; Iheka, 2018, 2021; Wenzel, 2019); and non-metropolitan philosophy, aesthetics, and publishing (e.g. Allan, 2016; El-Ariss, 2018; Etherington, 2017; Helgesson, 2022; Jackson, 2021; Krishnan, 2018; Mangharam, 2017). Crucially, although the scholars I have named here are nearly all based in metropolitan anglophone universities, they are in conversation with other readers not only in these locations. They speak about their work in settings beyond the university, they collaborate with writers and activists outside of the metropolitan centres, and they often work with languages other than English.

Above all, this book has tried to show that, although there is much left to be done, the work of decolonizing literary studies is already under way. This undertaking draws on the example of the mid-twentieth-century struggles for political and cultural decolonization across the former European colonies, but it also responds to the crises of the present moment, which grow out of past confrontations but take reconfigured forms. I hope that readers will feel encouraged and inspired to take part in the struggles that come next.

Notes

1 This is a more expansive definition than Tuck and Yang's influential – and controversial – proposal that the term 'decolonization' refers only to the return of colonized land, and that it should not be used as a 'metaphor' for any other social justice projects (2012, pp. 1–10). Gopal (2021, p. 885) rightly points out that their intervention applies specifically to North American settler-colonial contexts but is less helpful for confronting other sites of colonization.

2 In this book, I use both 'imperialism' and 'colonialism' to name formal practices of European rule over non-European locations, and both 'anti-imperialism' and 'anticolonialism' to name theories and practices of resistance to it. It can be useful to think of 'colonialism' as describing the practice of political and military domination and 'imperialism' as the expansionist – and, in the modern period, capitalist – ideology that underpins it.

3 This overview is based on a survey of degree outlines and module listings for autumn 2020 from a selection of English departments in the US, the UK, and Australia, drawing on information that is publicly available online. Institutions surveyed were, in the UK, Bristol, Cambridge, Durham, King's College London, Leeds, Manchester, Oxford, Queen Mary University of London, University College London, Warwick, York; in the US, Columbia, University of Colorado Boulder, Cornell, Harvard, New York University, Stanford, University of California at Berkeley, University of California Los Angeles, University of Virginia, University of Washington Seattle, Yale; and, in Australia, Adelaide, Melbourne, Monash, Sydney, University of New South Wales, University of Western Australia.

Notes to pages 36–60

4 The discussion that follows focuses on W. W. Norton's flagship anthologies, *The Norton Anthology of English Literature* and *The Norton Anthology of Poetry*. W. W. Norton also publishes anthologies that showcase the writing of US ethnic minority groups, including *When the Light of the World Was Subdued, Our Songs Came Through: A Norton Anthology of Native Nations Poetry* (Harjo, 2020), *The Norton Anthology of African-American Literature* (Gates and Smith, 2014), and *The Norton Anthology of Latino Literature* (Stavans, 2011), as well as *The Norton Anthology of World Literature* (Puchner, 2018).

5 It must be noted, however, that the 'Africanization' of the curriculum from the 1970s onwards in the University of Nairobi and other African universities has taken place alongside the progressive impoverishment of the university sector across the continent (cf. Nuttall, 2020).

6 Other important online resources from the UK context include the Pedagogies for Social Justice project, which recommends readings and other resources by discipline, including literature (University of Westminster, 2021); the 'Anti-Racist Curriculum Project guide' (AdvanceHE, 2020); and Project Myopia (n.d.).

7 For a useful discussion of the relationship of the term 'experimental' in twentieth-century American literature to concepts drawn from the history of science rather than a set of established formal criteria, see Cecire (2019).

8 For a fuller discussion and examples of efforts to put these principles in practice, see the work of the research networks Language Acts and Worldmaking (2022) and 'Multilingual locals and significant geographies' (SOAS, n.d.).

9 Apter subsequently changed her position in response to the growth of world literature studies in translation and advocated instead for the recognition of 'untranslatability' (Apter, 2013), as I will discuss later in this chapter.

10 I have retained Ngũgĩ's use of masculine pronouns in this passage.

11 See also my discussion of *Decolonising the Mind* in chapter 1. Simon Gikandi (2000) notes that Ngũgĩ's position on the use of English has softened over the decades of his political exile in the United States. Gikandi argues that this is partly because of the difficulty of publishing in an African language within Western institutions of knowledge, and partly because of Ngũgĩ's move away from the Marxism that informed his work in the 1960s and 1970s. For a more recent articulation

158 Notes to pages 73–114

of Ngũgĩ's self-conception as a 'language warrior', see Inani (2018).

12 For a discussion of the Israeli state's instrumentalization of Arabic-language learning within its 'security' apparatus, see Eyal (2006) and Mendel (2014).

13 For examples of Djebar's continuing influence in French and francophone literary studies, see Chikhi (2007) and Cercle des Amis d'Assia Djebar (2012).

14 For an account of the comparable but distinct multilingual landscape of Moroccan literature, see Laachir (2023).

15 For a critique of Djebar's failure to reckon with the presence of the Black servant in Delacroix's original painting (or with its minimization in Picasso's), see O'Beirne (2003).

16 For discussion of the work of Méchakra, Negrouche, and Rahmani, see Jarvis (2021). For a fuller list of Algerian men and women writers whose work is available in English, see Aoudjit (2017).

17 The FSLN was voted back into power in 2007 and remains the ruling party in Nicaragua at the time of writing, but the current incarnation of the party cannot be described as revolutionary (see Baltodano, 2006; La Botz, 2016).

18 Information about editions and translations of these texts is taken from worldcat.org.

19 For an assessment of the political aims and shortcomings of the PFLP hijackings, see Hobson (2020).

20 Here I have amended the published translation to be more faithful to the Spanish original: 'Ahora pienso en mi niñez. En el campo. En las campesinas que morían pariendo, en los que morían de hambre. De explotación, de miseria' (Tijerino and Randall, 1977, p. 84).

21 'Racial capitalism' – meaning the 'mutual dependence of capitalism and racism' (Kundnani, 2020) – is not a term that Davis uses in the original text of *An Autobiography*. However, she does use it in the introduction to the 2022 edition and elsewhere in her recent work (e.g. Davis, 2017), and it accurately describes her articulation of the relationship between anti-Black racism and capitalism throughout the autobiography. The term 'racial capitalism' is most closely associated with the work of the Black American political theorist Cedric Robinson, particularly his book *Black Marxism* (2000 [1983]).

22 For a more recent account of Davis's work on prison abolition, see Davis (2011).

Notes to pages 118–153

23 For a discussion of this tradition in China, see Laughlin (2002); in Central and Eastern Europe, Zubel (2017); and in the United States, Shulman (2000).

24 See e.g. the Cambridge Histories of Literature, which have a larger geographical range than the Cambridge Companions mentioned in chapter 2.

25 This is a particularly fraught debate in Arabic literary criticism, where some critics see the novel as a descendant of pre-colonial genres such as the *maqama*, a narrative form written in ornamental rhymed prose; others see it as a European genre that has been appropriated; and still others see it as a combination of the two. For summaries of these debates, see Allen (2007); Rastegar (2007); Siddiq (2007).

26 On the role of poetry in anticolonial and postcolonial anti-state struggles in the Arab world, particularly Palestine, see Alshaer (2014). On the role of Islamicate poetry in anti-state movements in South Asia, see Plys (2020).

27 Christopher Warnes's description of 'faith-based magical realism' is pertinent here: it calls 'upon the reader to suspend rational-empirical judgements about the way things are in favour of an expanded order of reality. Frequently, though not always, it does so in order to recuperate a non-western cultural world view' (2009, p. 12).

28 The Lakota and Dakota peoples are both part of the larger Indigenous American tribal confederacy known by outsiders as the Sioux.

29 For examples of this kind of scholarship in classics, see 'Comparative classics: Greece, Rome, and India' (University College London, n.d.) and the volume *Critical Ancient World Studies: The Case for Forgetting Classics* (Umachandran and Ward, forthcoming).

References

Abu-Manneh, B. (2016) *The Palestinian Novel: From 1948 to the Present*. Cambridge: Cambridge University Press.

Achebe, C. (1975) *Morning Yet on Creation Day*. Garden City, NY: Anchor Books.

—— (1978) 'An image of Africa', *Research in African Literatures*, 9(1): 1–15.

—— (1997 [1965]) 'English and the African writer', *Transition*, no. 75/76: 342–9

—— (2001 [1958]) *Things Fall Apart*. London: Penguin.

Adebisi, F. (2019) 'Decolonisation and the law school: initial thoughts', *African Skies*, https://folukeafrica.com /decolonisation-the-law-school-initial-thoughts [blog].

AdvanceHE (2020) 'Anti-Racist Curriculum Project guide', www.advance-he.ac.uk/anti-racist-curriculum-project /project-guide.

Alessandrini, A. (2010) 'Small places, now and then: Frantz Fanon, Jamaica Kincaid, and the futures of postcolonial criticism', *Journal of Postcolonial Writing*, 46(5): 553–64.

—— (2014) *Frantz Fanon and the Future of Cultural Politics: Finding Something Different*. Lanham, MD: Lexington Books.

—— (2023) *Decolonize Multiculturalism*. New York: OR Books.

Al-Jazeera (2018) 'France admits torture during Algeria's war of independence', 13 September, www.aljazeera.com/news /2018/9/13/france-admits-torture-during-algerias-war-of -independence.

References

Allan, M. (2016) *In the Shadow of World Literature: Sites of Reading in Colonial Egypt*. Princeton, NJ: Princeton University Press.

Allen, R. (2007) 'Rewriting literary history: the case of the Arabic novel', *Journal of Arabic Literature*, 38(3): 247–60.

Alshaer, A. (2014) *Poetry and Politics in the Modern Arab World*. London: Hurst.

Andrews, K. (2018) Preface, in R. Chantiluke, B. Kwoba, and A. Nkopo, eds, *Rhodes Must Fall: The Struggle to Decolonise the Racist Heart of Empire*. London: Zed Books.

Antena Aire (2020) *How to Build Language Justice*, http://antenaantena.org/wp-content/uploads/2021/04 /AntenaAire_HowToBuildLanguageJustice-2020.pdf.

Aoudjit, A. (2017) *Algerian Literature: A Reader's Guide and Anthology*. New York: Peter Lang.

Apter, E. (2006) *The Translation Zone: A New Comparative Literature*. Princeton, NJ: Princeton University Press.

— (2013) *Against World Literature: The Politics of Untranslatability*. London: Verso.

AQA Education (2021) *GCSE English Literature: Specification*, https://filestore.aqa.org.uk/resources/english /specifications/AQA-8702-SP-2015.PDF.

Ashcroft, B., Griffiths, G., and Tiffin, H. (2002 [1989]) *The Empire Writes Back: Theory and Practice in Post-Colonial Contexts*. 2nd edn, London: Routledge.

Attridge, D. (2004) *J. M. Coetzee & the Ethics of Reading*. Chicago: University of Chicago Press.

Azoulay, A. (2019) *Potential History: Unlearning Imperialism*. London: Verso.

Baker, M., ed. (2016) *Translating Dissent: Voices from and with the Egyptian Revolution*. London: Routledge.

Baltodano, M. (2006) 'Nicaragua: from Sandinismo to "Danielismo"', *International Socialist Review*, no. 50.

Baneth-Nouailhetas, E. (2008) 'Committed writing, committed writer?', in R. Ghosh and A. Navarro-Tejero, eds, *Globalizing Dissent: Essays on Arundhati Roy*. London: Routledge.

References

Barber, K. (2007) *The Anthropology of Texts, Persons, and Publics: Oral and Written Culture in Africa and Beyond.* Cambridge: Cambridge University Press.

Bassnett, S. (2013) 'Postcolonialism and/as translation', in G. Huggan, ed., *The Oxford Handbook of Postcolonial Studies.* Oxford: Oxford University Press.

Benjamin, W. (2019 [1955]) *Illuminations*, trans. H. Zohn. New York: Houghton Mifflin Harcourt.

Bernard, A. (2013) *Rhetorics of Belonging: Nation, Narration, and Israel/Palestine.* Liverpool: Liverpool University Press.

— (2014) 'Taking sides: Palestinian advocacy and metropolitan theatre', *Journal of Postcolonial Writing*, 50(2): 163–75.

Bhabha, H. K. (2004 [1994]) *The Location of Culture.* London: Routledge.

Bhanot, K. (2015) 'Decolonise, not diversify', https://mediadiversified.org/2015/12/30/is-diversity-is-only-for-white-people.

Boehmer, E. (1995) *Migrant Metaphors: Colonial and Postcolonial Literature.* Oxford: Oxford University Press.

— (1998) 'Questions of neo-orientalism', *Interventions*, 1(1): 18–21.

Boochani, B. (2018a) *A Letter from Manus Island*, trans. O. Tofighian. Adamstown, NSW, Australia: Borderstream Books.

— (2018b) *No Friend but the Mountains: The True Story of an Illegally Imprisoned Refugee*, trans. O. Tofighian. London: Picador.

Brathwaite, K. (1993 [1979/81]) 'History of the voice', in Brathwaite, *Roots*. Ann Arbor: University of Michigan Press.

Brennan, T. (2014) 'The case against irony', *Journal of Commonwealth Literature*, 49(3): 379–94.

— (2017) 'Homiletic realism', in E. Kent and T. Tomsky, eds, *Negative Cosmopolitanism: Cultures and Politics of World Citizenship after Globalization.* Montreal: McGill–Queen's University Press.

Brontë, C. (2006 [1847]) *Jane Eyre.* Harmondsworth: Penguin.

References 163

Byron, K. (2006) 'Doris Tijerino: revolution, writing, and resistance in Nicaragua', *NWSA Journal*, 18(3): 104–21.

Camus, A. (2006 [1957]) *Exile in the Kingdom*, trans. Carol Cosman. Harmondsworth: Penguin.

Cecire, N. (2019) *Experimental: American Literature and the Aesthetics of Knowledge*. Baltimore: Johns Hopkins University Press.

Centre for the Study of the Legacies of British Slavery (2022) 'Legacies of British slavery', www.ucl.ac.uk/lbs/.

Cercle des Amis d'Assia Djebar (2012) *Lire Assia Djebar!* Ciboure: La Cheminante.

Césaire, A. (1969) *Une tempête: d'après 'La tempête' de Shakespeare: adaptation pour un théâtre nègre*. Paris: Éditions du Seuil.

— (2000 [1955]) *Discourse on Colonialism*, trans. J. Pinkham. New York: Monthly Review Press.

— (2002 [1969]) *A Tempest*, trans. R. Miller. New York: Theatre Communications Group.

Chaudhuri, A., ed. (2001) *The Picador Book of Modern Indian Literature*. London: Picador.

Chikhi, B. (2007) *Assia Djebar: histoires et fantaisies*. Paris: Presses de l'Université de Paris-Sorbonne.

Cobham, R. (2002) '"Mwen na rien, Msieu": Jamaica Kincaid and the problem of creole gnosis', *Callaloo*, 25(3): 868–84.

Coetzee, J. M. (1987 [1986]) *Foe*. Harmondsworth: Penguin.

Comfort, S. (2008) 'How to tell a story to change the world: Arundhati Roy, globalization, and environmental feminism', in R. Ghosh and A. Navarro-Tejero, eds, *Globalizing Dissent: Essays on Arundhati Roy*. London: Routledge.

Conrad, J. (2008 [1899]) *Heart of Darkness and Other Tales*. Oxford: Oxford University Press.

Court, F. E. (1992) *Institutionalizing English Literature: The Culture and Politics of Literary Study, 1750–1900*. Stanford, CA: Stanford University Press.

Dabashi, H. (2013) 'Found in translation', *New York Times*, 28 July, https://opinionator.blogs.nytimes.com/2013/07/28/found-in-translation/.

Damrosch, D., and Pike, D., eds (2009) *The Longman Anthology of World Literature*. 2nd edn, London: Pearson/ Longman.

Dao, A., and Boochani, B. (2020) 'Interview: André Dao and Behrouz Boochani', *Law Text Culture*, 24: 50–9.

Davis, A. (2011) *Abolition Democracy: Beyond Empire, Prisons, and Torture*. New York: Seven Stories Press.

—— (2017) 'An interview on the futures of black radicalism', in G. T. Johnson and A. Lubin, eds, *Futures of Black Radicalism*. London: Verso.

—— (2022 [1974]) *An Autobiography*. London: Penguin.

De'Ath, A. (2019) 'The rejection of closure': lecture for 'Writing Race, Writing Gender', King's College London.

—— (2020) Interview with the author, 15 October.

Deckard, S. (2020) 'Water shocks: neoliberal hydrofiction and the crisis of "cheap water"', in S. Gunne and N. Lazarus, eds, *The World-Literary System and the Atlantic*. London: Routledge.

—— (2021) 'Gendering petrofiction: energy, imperialism, and social reproduction', in S. Balkan and S. Nandi, eds, *Oil Fictions: World Literature and Our Contemporary Petrosphere*. Philadelphia: Pennsylvania State University Press.

Djebar, A. (1980) *Femmes d'Alger dans leur appartement*. Paris: Des Femmes.

—— (1992) *Women of Algiers in their Apartment*, trans. M. de Jager. Charlottesville: University of Virginia Press.

Doward, J. (2020) 'I've been unfairly targeted, says academic at heart of National Trust "woke" row', *The Guardian*, 20 December, www.theguardian.com/uk-news/2020/dec/20/ive-been-unfairly-targeted-says-academic-at-heart-of-national-trust-woke-row.

Dyssou, N. (2017) 'An interview with Ngũgĩ wa Thiong'o', *Los Angeles Review of Books*, 23 April, https://lareviewofbooks.org/article/an-interview-with-ngugi-wa-thiongo.

Eagleton, T. (1996 [1983]) *Literary Theory: An Introduction*. 2nd edn, Oxford: Blackwell.

El-Ariss, T. (2018) *Leaks, Hacks, and Scandals: Arab Culture in the Digital Age.* Princeton, NJ: Princeton University Press.

Elmarsafy, Z., Bernard, A., and Attwell, D., eds (2013) *Debating Orientalism.* Basingstoke: Palgrave Macmillan.

Etherington, B. (2016) 'An answer to the question: What is decolonization? Frantz Fanon's *The Wretched of the Earth* and Jean-Paul Sartre's *Critique of Dialectical Reason*', *Modern Intellectual History*, 13(1): 151–78.

—— (2017) *Literary Primitivism.* Stanford, CA: Stanford University Press.

—— (2018) 'Scales, systems, and meridians', in B. Etherington and J. Zimbler, eds, *The Cambridge Companion to World Literature.* Cambridge: Cambridge University Press.

Etherington, B., and Zimbler, J. (2014) 'Field, material, technique: on renewing postcolonial literary criticism', *Journal of Commonwealth Literature*, 49(3): 279–97.

—— (2021) 'Decolonize practical criticism?', *English: Journal of the English Association*, 70(270): 227–36.

Etherington, B., Zimbler, J., and Bower, R. (2014) 'Crafts of world literature: field, material, and translation', *Journal of Commonwealth Literature*, 49(3): 273–8.

Euro-Med Human Rights Monitor (2022) 'Europe's official, media handling of Ukrainian crisis exposes deep-rooted, racist policy against non-Europeans', 2 March, https://euromedmonitor.org/en/article/4934/Europe%27s-official, -media-handling-of-Ukrainian-crisis-exposes-deep-rooted, -racist-policy-against-non-Europeans.

Eyal, G. (2006) *The Disenchantment of the Orient: Expertise in Arab Affairs and the Israeli State.* Stanford, CA: Stanford University Press.

Falci, E. (2020) *The Value of Poetry.* Cambridge: Cambridge University Press.

Fanon, F. (1963) *The Wretched of the Earth*, trans. C. Farringdon. New York: Grove Press.

—— (2018) *Alienation and Freedom*, ed. J. Khalfa and R. Young, trans. S. Corcoran. London: Bloomsbury.

Featherstone, D. (2012) *Solidarity: Hidden Histories and Geographies of Internationalism.* London: Zed Books.

Fehskens, E. M. (2018) 'The epic hero in Wilson Harris's

Palace of the Peacock', *Journal of Modern Literature*, 41(4): 90–106.

Ferguson, M., Kendall, T., and Salter, M. J., eds (2018) *The Norton Anthology of Poetry*. 6th edn, New York: W. W. Norton.

Fly Cambridge (2017) 'Decolonising the English Faculty: an open letter', https://cambridgefly.wordpress.com/2017/06/14/decolonising-the-english-faculty-an-open-letter.

Forsdick, C. (2018) 'Literature and decolonization', in M. Thomas and A. S. Thompson, eds, *The Oxford Handbook of the Ends of Empire*. Oxford: Oxford University Press.

Fowler, C. (2021) *Green Unpleasant Land: Creative Responses to Rural England's Colonial Connections*. Leeds: Peepal Tree Press.

—— (2023) *The Countryside: Ten Walks Through Colonial Britain*. London: Allen Lane.

Freeman, J. (2017) 'Why you should be reading poet Layli Long Soldier', *Los Angeles Times*, 5 May, www.latimes.com/books/jacketcopy/la-ca-jc-layli-long-soldier-20170426-story.html.

Fuchs, F. (2020) 'Novelizing non-fiction: Arundhati Roy's *Walking with the Comrades* and the critical realism of global anglophone literature', *Interventions*, 23(8): 1187–1203.

Gardiner, M. (2013) *The Constitution of English Literature: The State, the Nation and the Canon*. London: Bloomsbury.

Gates, H. L., and Smith, V., eds (2014) *The Norton Anthology of African-American Literature*. 3rd edn, New York: W. W. Norton.

Getachew, A., and Mantena, K. (2021) 'Anticolonialism and the decolonization of political theory', *Critical Times*, 4(3): 359–88.

Gikandi, S. (2000) 'Traveling theory: Ngugi's return to English', *Research in African Literatures*, 31(2): 194–209.

Gilmour, R. (2020) *Bad English*. Manchester: Manchester University Press.

Goebel, W., and Schabio, S., eds (2012) *Locating Postcolonial Narrative Genres*. London: Routledge.

References

Gopal, P. (2009) *The Indian English Novel: Nation, History, and Narration*. Oxford: Oxford University Press.

—— (2019) *Insurgent Empire: Anticolonial Resistance and British Dissent*. London: Verso.

—— (2021) 'On decolonisation and the university', *Textual Practice*, 35(6): 873–99.

Gorky, M. (2020 [1906]) *The Mother*, trans. H. Aplin. Richmond, Surrey: Alma Books.

Graff, G. (2007 [1987]) *Professing Literature: An Institutional History*. 2nd edn, Chicago: University of Chicago Press.

Greenblatt, S., ed. (2018) *The Norton Anthology of English Literature*. 10th edn, New York: W. W. Norton.

Griffis, R. (2020) '"Language to reach with": Layli Long Soldier's *WHEREAS* connects words to reality', *Studies in American Indian Literatures*, 32(1/2): 52–74.

Hansen, M. (2016) '"A world of something": Jamaica Kincaid and the new global epic', *Comparative Literature*, 68(1): 31–45.

Harjo, J., ed. (2020) *When the Light of the World Was Subdued, Our Songs Came Through: A Norton Anthology of Native Nations Poetry*. New York: W. W. Norton.

Harlow, B. (1987) *Resistance Literature*. London: Methuen.

—— (1996) *After Lives: Legacies of Revolutionary Writing*. London: Verso.

Harris, W. (2021 [1960]) *Palace of the Peacock*. London: Faber & Faber.

Harrison, N. (2015) 'Notes on translation as research', *Modern Languages Open*, http://doi.org/10.3828/mlo.v0i0.78.

Harrison, O. (2015) *Transcolonial Maghreb: Imagining Palestine in the Era of Decolonization*. Stanford, CA: Stanford University Press.

—— (2023) *Natives against Nativism: Antiracism and Indigenous Critique in Postcolonial France*. Minneapolis: University of Minnesota Press.

Hartman, A. (2015) *A War for the Soul of America: A History of the Culture Wars*. Chicago: University of Chicago Press.

References

Helgesson, S. (2022) *Decolonisations of Literature: Critical Practice in Africa and Brazil after 1945*. Liverpool: Liverpool University Press.

Hiddleston, J. (2006) *Assia Djebar: Out of Algeria*. Liverpool: Liverpool University Press.

Hitchcock, P. (2003) 'The genre of postcoloniality', *New Literary History*, 34(2): 299–330.

—— (2017) 'Counter-fitting', *Cambridge Journal of Postcolonial Literary Inquiry*, 4(2): 159–75.

Hobson, A. (2020) 'Creating a world stage: revolution airport and the illusion of power', *International History Review*, 42(5): 930–50.

hooks, b. (1994) *Teaching to Transgress: Education as the Practice of Freedom*. London: Routledge.

Hoover, E. (2017) 'Slippery language of apology captured in poetic forms', *Star Tribune*, 27 August.

Huddart, D. (2006) *Homi K. Bhabha*. London: Routledge.

Huggan, G., ed. (2013) *The Oxford Handbook of Postcolonial Studies*. Oxford: Oxford University Press.

Huxtable, S.-A., Fowler, C., Kefalas, C., and Slocombe, E., eds (2020) *Interim Report on the Connections between Colonialism and Properties now in the Care of the National Trust, including Links with Historic Slavery*, https://nt.global.ssl.fastly.net/binaries/content/assets/website/national/pdf/colonialism-and-historic-slavery-report.pdf.

Iheka, C. (2018) *Naturalizing Africa: Ecological Violence, Agency, and Postcolonial Resistance in African Literature*. Cambridge: Cambridge University Press.

—— (2021) *African Ecomedia: Network Forms, Planetary Politics*. Durham, NC: Duke University Press.

Inani, R. (2018) 'Language is a "war zone": a conversation with Ngũgĩ wa Thiong'o', *The Nation*, 9 March, www.thenation.com/article/archive/language-is-a-war-zone-a-conversation-with-ngugi-wa-thiongo.

Irving, S. (2012) *Leila Khaled: Icon of Palestinian Liberation*. London: Pluto Press.

Jackson, J.-M. (2021) *The African Novel of Ideas: Philosophy and Individualism in the Age of Global Writing*. Princeton, NJ: Princeton University Press.

References   169

Jameson, F. (1986) 'Third-world literature in the era of multinational capitalism', *Social Text*, no. 15: 65–88.

Jarvis, J. (2021) *Decolonizing Memory: Algeria and the Politics of Testimony*. Durham, NC: Duke University Press.

Jawad, R. (2014) 'Aren't we human? Normalizing Palestinian performances', *Arab Studies Journal*, 22(1): 28–45.

Jayawardane, M. N., and Walcott, R. (2021) 'Diversity efforts in universities are nothing but façade painting', *Al-Jazeera*, 7 May, www.aljazeera.com/opinions/2021/5/7/diversity-efforts-in-universities-are-nothing-but-facade-painting.

Kachru, B. (2006 [1990]) 'The alchemy of English', in B. Ashcroft, G. Griffiths, and H. Tiffin, eds, *The Post-Colonial Studies Reader*. 2nd edn, London: Routledge.

Kanafani, G. (1968) 'Resistance literature in occupied Palestine', *Afro-Asian Writings*, 1(2–3): 65–79.

—— (1978 [1963]) *Men in the Sun [Rijal fi al-shams]*, trans. H. Kilpatrick. Washington, DC: Three Continents Press.

Kennedy, N., and Mortensen, A. (2021) 'Record number of people attempt to cross the border between Poland and Belarus, officials say', CNN, 11 October, https://edition.cnn.com/2021/10/10/europe/poland-belarus-border-crossing-migrants-record-number-intl/index.html.

Khaled, L. (1973) *My People Shall Live: Autobiography of a Revolutionary*. London: Hodder & Stoughton.

Kilolo, M., ed. (2016) 'Translation issue 01: Ngũgĩ wa Thiong'o', *Jalada*, 22 March, https://jaladaafrica.org/2016/03/22/jalada-translation-issue-01-ngugi-wa-thiongo.

Kincaid, J. (1985 [1983]) *At the Bottom of the River*. New York: Random House.

—— (1988) *A Small Place*. New York: Farrar, Strauss, Giroux.

Knepper, W., and Deckard, S. (2016) 'Towards a radical world literature: experimental writing in a globalizing world', *ARIEL*, 47(1/2): 1–25.

Knights, B. (2017) *Pedagogic Criticism: Reconfiguring University English Studies*. Basingstoke: Palgrave Macmillan.

Krishnan, M. (2018) *Contingent Canons: African Literature*

and the Politics of Location. Cambridge: Cambridge University Press.

— (2019) 'Notes for "Workshop on Decolonization"', shared with the author.

Kundnani, A. (2020) 'What is racial capitalism?', 23 October, www.kundnani.org/what-is-racial-capitalism/ [blog].

La Botz, D. (2016) *What Went Wrong? The Nicaraguan Revolution: A Marxist Analysis.* Leiden: Brill.

Laachir, K. (2023) *The Postcolonial Moroccan Novel in Arabic and French.* Edinburgh: Edinburgh University Press.

Laachir, K., Marzagora, S., and Orsini, F. (2018) 'Multilingual locals and significant geographies: for a ground-up and located approach to world literature', *Modern Languages Open,* www.modernlanguagesopen.org/articles/10.3828/mlo.v0i0.190/.

Language Acts and Worldmaking (2022) https://languageacts.org.

Laughlin, C. A. (2002) *Chinese Reportage: The Aesthetics of Historical Experience.* Durham, NC: Duke University Press.

Lazali, K. (2018) *Le trauma colonial: une enquête sur les effets psychiques et politiques contemporains de l'oppression coloniale en Algérie.* Paris: La Découverte.

Lazarus, N., ed. (2004) *The Cambridge Companion to Postcolonial Literary Studies.* Cambridge: Cambridge University Press.

— (2011) *The Postcolonial Unconscious.* Cambridge: Cambridge University Press.

— (2013) '"Third worldism" and the political imaginary of postcolonial studies', in G. Huggan, ed., *The Oxford Handbook of Postcolonial Studies.* Oxford: Oxford University Press.

Lee, C. J., ed. (2010) *Making a World after Empire: The Bandung Moment and its Political Afterlives.* Athens: Ohio University Press.

Linke, G. (2019) 'Radical resistance: constructions of a transnational self in Angela Davis's and Cynthia McKinney's memoirs', *Journal of Transnational American Studies,* 10(1).

References

Loh, L. (2013) *The Postcolonial Country in Contemporary Literature*. Basingstoke: Palgrave Macmillan.

LoLordo, V. N. (2004) 'Identity poetics? or, *The Norton Anthology of Modern and Contemporary Poetry*', *Postmodern Culture*, 15(1).

Long Soldier, L. (2019 [2017]) *Whereas*. London: Picador.

Loomba, A. (1998) *Colonialism/Postcolonialism*. London: Routledge.

Macey, D. (2012) *Frantz Fanon: A Biography*. London: Verso.

McLeod, J. (2013) 'Postcolonialism and literature', in G. Huggan, ed., *The Oxford Handbook of Postcolonial Studies*. Oxford: Oxford University Press.

Majumder, A. (2020) *Insurgent Imaginations: World Literature and the Periphery*. Cambridge: Cambridge University Press.

Mangharam, M. L. (2017) *Literatures of Liberation: Non-European Universalisms and Democratic Progress*. Athens: Ohio State University Press.

Mannoni, O. (1950) *Psychologie de la colonisation*. Paris: Éditions du Seuil.

Marcetic, B. (2022) 'Occupied Palestine is as entitled to the world's solidarity as occupied Ukraine', *Jacobin*, 19 April, https://jacobinmag.com/2022/04/palestine-israel-occupation-solidarity-ukraine-russia-al-aqsa-mosque.

Mardorossian, C. (1999) 'Shutting up the subaltern: silences, stereotypes, and double-entendre in Jean Rhys's *Wide Sargasso Sea*', *Callaloo*, 22(4): 1071–90.

Marx, J. (2004) 'Postcolonial literature and the Western literary canon', in N. Lazarus, ed., *The Cambridge Companion to Postcolonial Literary Studies*. Cambridge: Cambridge University Press.

Mbembe, A. (2015) 'Decolonizing knowledge and the question of the archive', Platform for Experimental Collaborative Ethnography, https://worldpece.org/content/mbembe-achille-2015-%E2%80%9Cdecolonizing-knowledge-and-question-archive%E2%80%9D-africa-country.

Melamed, J. (2011) *Represent and Destroy: Rationalizing Violence in the New Racial Capitalism*. Minneapolis: University of Minnesota Press.

Mendel, Y. (2014) *The Creation of Israeli Arabic: Security and Politics in Arabic Studies in Israel*. Basingstoke: Palgrave Macmillan.

Mignolo, W. (2011) *The Darker Side of Western Modernity: Global Futures, Decolonial Options*. Durham, NC: Duke University Press.

Mignolo, W., and Walsh, C. E. (2018) *On Decoloniality: Concepts, Analytics, Praxis*. Durham, NC: Duke University Press.

Mohammad, A. (2014) 'Theatre of the occupied', *Wasafiri*, 29(4): 24–9.

Moore-Gilbert, B. (2000) 'Spivak and Bhabha', in H. Schwarz and S. Ray, eds, *A Companion to Postcolonial Studies*. Oxford: Blackwell.

Morreira, S., and Luckett, K. (2018) 'Questions academics can ask to decolonise their classrooms', *The Conversation*, 17 October, https://theconversation.com/questions-academics-can-ask-to-decolonise-their-classrooms-103251.

Morton, S. (2002) *Gayatri Chakravorty Spivak*. London: Routledge.

Moss, S. (2015) 'Palestinian playwright Dalia Taha: "You want stories of suffering"', *The Guardian*, 22 February, www.theguardian.com/stage/2015/feb/22/dalia-taha-fireworks-interview.

Moyn, S. (2010) *The Last Utopia: Human Rights in History*. Cambridge, MA: Harvard University Press.

Mufti, A. (2016) *Forget English! Orientalisms and World Literatures*. Cambridge, MA: Harvard University Press.

Mullaney, J. (2002) '"Globalizing dissent"? Arundhati Roy, local and postcolonial feminisms in the transnational economy', *World Literature Written in English*, 40(1): 56–70.

Mullen, H. (1992) *S*PeRM**K*T*. Philadelphia: Singing Horse Press.

Nassar, T. (2022) 'Israel destroys Sheikh Jarrah home in cruel and criminal act', *The Electronic Intifada*, 19 January, https://electronicintifada.net/blogs/tamara-nassar/israel-destroys-sheikh-jarrah-home-cruel-and-criminal-act.

Nasta, S. (2009) '"Beyond the frame": writing a life and

References 173

Jamaica Kincaid's family album', *Contemporary Women's Writing*, 3(1): 64–86.

National Trust (n.d.) 'Colonial countryside project', www.nationaltrust.org.uk/who-we-are/research/colonial-countryside-project.

Nayar, P. K. (2017) 'Mobility and insurgent celebrityhood: the case of Arundhati Roy', *Open Cultural Studies*, 1(1): 46–54.

Ngũgĩ wa Thiong'o (1986) *Decolonising the Mind: The Politics of Language in African Literature*. Woodbridge, Suffolk: James Currey.

Ngũgĩ wa Thiong'o, Owuor Anyumba, H., and Lo Liyong, T. (1972 [1968]) 'On the abolition of the English department', in Ngũgĩ wa Thiong'o, *Homecoming: Essays on African and Caribbean Literature, Culture and Politics*. London: Heinemann.

Niblett, M. (2013) 'The "impossible quest for wholeness": sugar, cassava, and the ecological aesthetic in *The Guyana Quartet*', *Journal of Postcolonial Writing*, 49(2): 148–60.

Niranjana, T. (1992) *Siting Translation: History, Post-Structuralism, and the Colonial Context*. Berkeley: University of California Press.

Nixon, R. (1987) 'Caribbean and African appropriations of *The Tempest*', *Critical Inquiry*, 13(3): 557–78.

—— (2011) *Slow Violence and the Environmentalism of the Poor*. Cambridge, MA: Harvard University Press.

Nuttall, S. (2020) 'The redistributed university', *The WISER Podcast*, https://witswiser.podbean.com/e/sarah-nuttall-the-redistributed-university/.

O'Beirne, E. (2003) 'Veiled vision: Assia Djebar on Delacroix, Picasso, and the *Femmes D'Alger*', *Romance Studies*, 21(1): 39–51.

Parry, B. (1987) 'Problems in current theories of colonial discourse', *Oxford Literary Review*, 9(1/2): 27–58.

—— (2004) *Postcolonial Studies: A Materialist Critique*. London: Routledge.

—— (2010) 'Countercurrents and tensions in Said's critical practice', in A. Iskander and H. Rustom, eds, *Edward*

Said: A Legacy of Emancipation and Representation. Berkeley: University of California Press.

Perkins, M. (2000) *Autobiography as Activism: Three Black Women of the Sixties.* Jackson: University of Mississippi Press.

Philip, M. N. (2015 [1989]) *She Tries Her Tongue/Her Silence Softly Breaks.* Middletown, CT: Wesleyan University Press.

Plys, K. (2020) 'The poetry of resistance: poetry as solidarity in postcolonial anti-authoritarian movements in Islamicate South Asia', *Theory, Culture & Society,* 37(7/8): 295–313.

Ponsford, D. (2017) 'Telegraph corrects story saying Cambridge University would drop white authors from reading lists', *Press Gazette,* 26 October, https://pressgazette.co.uk/publishers/nationals/telegraph-corrects-story-saying-cambridge-university-would-drop-white-authors-from-reading-lists/.

Pratt, M. L. (1993) *Imperial Eyes: Travel Writing and Transculturation.* London: Routledge.

Pravinchandra, S. (2018) 'Short story and peripheral production', in B. Etherington and J. Zimbler, eds, *The Cambridge Companion to World Literature.* Cambridge: Cambridge University Press.

Project Myopia (n.d.) https://projectmyopia.com.

Puchner, M., ed. (2018) *The Norton Anthology of World Literature.* 4th edn, New York: W. W. Norton.

Quijano, A. (2000) 'Coloniality of power, Eurocentrism, and Latin America', *Nepantla: Views from South,* 1(3): 533–80.

Rabea, R. A., and Almahameed, N. A. (2018) 'Genre crossing in Jamaica Kincaid's "Girl": from short fiction to poetry', *Advances in Language and Literary Studies,* 9(3): 157–65.

Ramazani, J., Ellman, R., and O'Clair, R., eds (2003) *The Norton Anthology of Modern and Contemporary Poetry.* 3rd edn, New York: W. W. Norton.

Rao, N. (2008) 'The politics of genre and the rhetoric of radical cosmopolitanism; or, Who's afraid of Arundhati Roy?', *Prose Studies,* 30(2): 159–76.

Rastegar, K. (2007) *Literary Modernity between the Middle East and Europe: Textual Transactions in*

References

Nineteenth-Century Arabic, English, and Persian Literatures. London: Routledge.

Rebaka, R. (2015) *The Negritude Movement: W. E. B. DuBois, Léon Damas, Aimé Césaire, Léopold Senghor, Frantz Fanon, and the Evolution of an Insurgent Idea.* Lanham, MD: Lexington Books.

Reed, A. (2014) *Freedom Time: The Poetics and Politics of Black Experimental Writing.* Baltimore: Johns Hopkins University Press.

Rhys, J. (1997 [1966]) *Wide Sargasso Sea.* Harmondsworth: Penguin.

Rivera Cusicanqui, S. (2020) *Ch'ixinakax utwixa: On Decolonising Practices and Discourses,* trans. M. Geidel. Cambridge: Polity.

Robinson, C. (2000 [1983]) *Black Marxism: The Making of the Black Radical Tradition.* Chapel Hill: University of North Carolina Press.

Roy, A. (1997) *The God of Small Things.* New York: HarperCollins.

— (2014) *Capitalism: A Ghost Story.* Chicago: Haymarket Books.

— (2016) *The End of Imagination.* Chicago: Haymarket Books.

— (2017) *The Ministry of Utmost Happiness.* London: Hamish Hamilton.

Rushdie, S. (1982) 'The empire writes back with a vengeance', *The Times,* 3 July.

Rushdie, S., and West, E., eds (1997) *The Vintage Book of Indian Writing 1947–1997.* New York: Vintage.

Saha, P. (2019) *An Empire of Touch: Women's Political Labor and the Fabrication of East Bengal.* New York: Columbia University Press.

Said, E. (1978) *Orientalism.* London: Penguin.

— (1994 [1993]) *Culture and Imperialism.* New York: Vintage.

— (2004) *Humanism and Democratic Criticism.* New York: Columbia University Press.

Sajjad, T. (2022) 'Ukrainian refugees are welcomed with open arms – not so with people fleeing other war-torn countries',

The Conversation, 9 March, https://theconversation.com/ukrainian-refugees-are-welcomed-with-open-arms-not-so-with-people-fleeing-other-war-torn-countries-178491.

Salih, T. (1991 [1966]) *Season of Migration to the North* [*Mawsim al-hijra ila al-shamal*], trans. D. Johnson-Davies. London: Heinemann.

Sanderson, S. (2022) 'Ukrainian refugees receive warm welcome in Calais – while other migrants remain marginalized', *InfoMigrants*, 10 March, www.infomigrants.net/en/post/39095/ukrainian-refugees-receive-warm-welcome-in-calais--while-other-migrants-remain-marginalized.

Scott, D. (2004) *Conscripts of Modernity: The Tragedy of Colonial Enlightenment*. Durham, NC: Duke University Press.

Shakespeare, W. (n.d. [1610/11]) *The Tempest*, ed. B. Mowat and P. Werstine. Folger Shakespeare Library, https://shakespeare.folger.edu.

Shankar, S. (2012) *Flesh and Fish Blood: Postcolonialism, Translation, and the Vernacular*. Berkeley: University of California Press.

Shesgreen, S. (2009) 'Canonizing the canonizer: a short history of *The Norton Anthology of English Literature*', *Critical Inquiry*, 35(2): 293–318.

Shulman, R. (2000) *The Power of Political Art: The 1930s Literary Left Reconsidered*. Chapel Hill: University of North Carolina Press.

Siddiq, M. (2007) *Arab Culture and the Novel: Genre, Identity, and Agency in Egyptian Fiction*. London: Routledge.

SOAS (2018) 'Decolonising SOAS: learning and teaching toolkit', https://blogs.soas.ac.uk/decolonisingsoas/learning-teaching/toolkit-for-programme-and-module-convenors.

SOAS (n.d.) 'Multilingual locals and significant geographies', http://mulosige.soas.ac.uk.

Sorensen, E. P. (2010) *Postcolonial Studies and the Literary: Theory, Interpretation and the Novel*. Basingstoke: Palgrave Macmillan.

—— (2021) *Postcolonial Realism and the Concept of the Political*. London: Routledge.

References

Spivak, G. C. (1985) 'Three women's texts and a critique of imperialism', *Critical Inquiry*, 12(1): 243–61.

—— (1987) *In Other Worlds: Essays in Cultural Politics*. London: Routledge.

—— (1988 [1985]) 'Can the subaltern speak?' in C. Nelson and L. Grossberg, eds, *Marxism and the Interpretation of Culture*. London: Macmillan.

—— (1990) 'Theory in the margin: Coetzee's Foe, reading Defoe's "Crusoe/Roxana"', *English in Africa*, 17(2): 1–23.

—— (2000) 'The politics of translation', in L. Venuti, ed., *The Translation Studies Reader*. London: Routledge.

—— (2003) *Death of a Discipline*. New York: Columbia University Press.

—— (2009 [1993]) *Outside in the Teaching Machine*. London: Routledge.

Stavans, I., ed. (2011) *The Norton Anthology of Latino Literature*. New York: W. W. Norton.

Stosuy, B. (2021) 'On overcoming the anxiety of making creative work', *The Creative Independent*, 27 April, https://thecreativeindependent.com/people/layli-long-soldier-on-poetry-as-prayer.

Sundorph, E. (2020) *Missing Pages: Increasing Diversity in the Literature We Teach*, www.teachfirst.org.uk/sites/default/files/2020-09/Missing%20Pages%20Report.pdf.

Taha, D. (2015a) *Fireworks*, trans. C. Naylor. London: Bloomsbury.

—— (2015b [2012]) *Keffiyeh/Made in China*, in N. Wallace and I. Khalidi, eds, *Inside/Outside: Six Plays from Palestine and the Diaspora*. New York: Theatre Communications Group.

Taha, D., and Twyman, R. (2015) 'The big idea: in conversation with Dalia Taha and Richard Twyman', Royal Court Theatre, 20 March, www.youtube.com/watch?v=G4oYl0RrlBA.

Tijerino, D., and Randall, M. (1977) *Somos millones: la vida de Doris María, combatiente nicaragüense*. Mexico City: Extemporaneos.

—— (1978) *Inside the Nicaraguan Revolution*, trans. E. Randall. Vancouver: New Star Books.

References

Tuck, E., and Yang, K. W. (2012) 'Decolonization is not a metaphor', *Decolonization: Indigeneity, Education & Society*, 1(1): 1–40.

Tuhiwai Smith, L. (2012 [1999]) *Decolonizing Methodologies: Research and Indigenous Peoples*. 2nd edn, London: Zed Books.

Turner, C. (2017) 'Cambridge to "decolonise" English literature', *Daily Telegraph*, 24 October, www.telegraph.co.uk/education/2017/10/24/cambridge-decolonise-english-literature.

Ufberg, M. (2022) '"It's happening now": how rising sea levels are causing a US migration crisis', *The Guardian*, 7 April, www.theguardian.com/environment/2022/apr/07/its-happening-now-how-rising-sea-levels-are-causing-a-us-migration-crisis.

Umachandran, M., and Ward, M., eds (forthcoming) *Critical Ancient World Studies: The Case for Forgetting Classics*.

University College London (n.d.) 'Comparative classics: Greece, Rome, and India', www.ucl.ac.uk/classics/research/research-projects/comparative-classics-greece-rome-and-india.

University of Westminster (2021) 'Reading lists: pedagogies for social justice', https://blog.westminster.ac.uk/psj/tools/reading-lists/.

US Congress (2009) S.J.Res. 14 – 111th Congress: A joint resolution to acknowledge a long history of official depredations and ill-conceived policies by the federal government regarding Indian tribes and offer an apology to all native peoples on behalf of the United States, www.congress.gov/bill/111th-congress/senate-joint-resolution/14/text.

Varma, R. (2021) 'Essaying solidarity: "Kaamraid" Roy and the politics of representation', *Modern Fiction Studies*, 67(2): 366–89.

Viswanathan, G. (2014 [1989]) *Masks of Conquest: Literary Study and British Rule in India*. New York: Columbia University Press.

Ward, J. (2020) 'The abolitionist curriculum', https://abolitionistcurriculum.wordpress.com.

—— (2021) Interview with the author, 3 March.

References

179

Warnes, C. (2009) *Magical Realism and the Postcolonial Novel: Between Faith and Irreverence*. Basingstoke: Palgrave Macmillan.

Welch, J. (1994) *Killing Custer: The Battle of the Little Bighorn and the Fate of the Plains Indians*. New York: W. W. Norton.

Wenzel, J. (2017) 'Decolonization', in I. Szeman, S. Blacker, and J. Sully, eds, *A Companion to Critical and Cultural Theory*. Chichester: Wiley-Blackwell.

—— (2019) *The Disposition of Nature: Environmental Crisis and World Literature*. New York: Fordham University Press.

Westall, C. (2015) 'Capitalizing on English literature: disciplinarity, academic labor and postcolonial studies', in A. Bernard, Z. Elmarsafy, and S. Murray, eds, *What Postcolonial Theory Doesn't Say*. London: Routledge.

WReC (Warwick Research Collective) (2015) *Combined and Uneven Development: Towards a New Theory of World-Literature*. Liverpool: Liverpool University Press.

Young, R. (2001) *Postcolonialism: An Historical Introduction*. Oxford: Blackwell.

—— (2020 [2003]) *Postcolonialism: A Very Short Introduction*. 2nd edn, Oxford: Oxford University Press.

Zimbler, J. (2014) *J. M. Coetzee and the Politics of Style*. Cambridge: Cambridge University Press.

Zubel, M. (2017) *Literary Reportage and the Politics of Cold War Internationalism*, dissertation, University of Minnesota.

Index

Page numbers in **bold** refer to 'reflection' and 'summary' boxes

'abolitionist curriculum' project 50–2
access to literature 47, 50, 58–9, 74, 154
Achebe, Chinua 21, 37
  and language 56, 58–9, 67
  and reading 79, 82, 87–8, **92**
activism 155
  author activism 105–6, 114, 117, 120–1
  Black activism 49, 51
  and colonialism 1–3, 78, 152–3
  Palestinian 31, 45, 46, 104, 108, 152–3
Adebisi, Foluke 1, 9
Adichie, Chimamanda 37, 38
African languages **32**, 39, 62, **63**, 65–6, 72, 89
  Gĩkũyũ 29, 59–60
  and Ngũgĩ wa Thiong'o 30, **32**, 56, 59–60, **63**, 157n11
  Swahili 39, 89
African literature
  and language of choice 29–30, **32**, 58–60, 62, 72

and universities 39, 157n5
African-Caribbean cultural heritage 139–41
  and language 56, 63–9, 139
  'nation language' 66, **68**, **69**
Algeria 93–5, 99, 100, **101**
Algerian women 81, 94, 97–100, **101**
Ambani, Mukesh 119–20
ambivalence 20, **25**
anaphora 27, 144–5
'ancestor respect' 138
Andrews, Kehinde 151, 153
Anglocentrism 70
anglophone literature 21, 23, 142
  and comparative literature 78, 83
  Indian 56, 61
  and language 58–69, 76
  and readership 30, 31, 61, 130–1, **135**
  see also Caribbean English/creole
anthologies 36–8, **41**, 61
anti-capitalism 27, 87, 103, 115, 137

Index

anticolonialism 78–101
anticolonial struggle/
  resistance 19, 30, **32**,
  78, 102–26
  and genre 128, 133,
  136–50
  definition 7, 156n2
anti-globalization 117
Antigua 137
anti-imperialism 7, 27, 137
anti-imperial struggle/
  resistance 30, 78, 92
  definition 156n2
'Anti-Racist Curriculum Project
  guide' 157n6
Anyumba, Henry Owuor 33,
  39, 40–3
Apologies, government 142,
  144–5
Apter, Emily 55, 56, 71, 157n9
Arabic 94–5
  language 100, 136
Argüello, Patrick 108
Ashcroft, Bill 79
Asociación de Mujeres
  Nicaragüenses Luisa
  Amanda Espinoza
  (AMNLAE) 105
assimilation 23, 28
At the Bottom of the River
  (Kincaid) 136, 138,
  139–40, 141
Attridge, Derek 83
Austen, Jane 17
Australia 116, 144
  Manus Island 116, 121, 123,
  124–5
authors, great 4
  see also texts, canonical
autobiography 122
  women's autobiographies
  104–14
  and capitalism 110, 112,
  158n21

and liberation movements
  108, 112–13
and violence against
  women 107–8, 110–11
Autobiography of My Mother
  (Kincaid) 141
autonomy, aesthetic 13–14,
  16
'avant-garde' 47–8
awareness 113, 114, 118,
  153–4
Azoulay, Ariella 8

Baker, Mona 75
Barber, Karin 132, 133
Benjamin, Walter 55
Bennett, Louise (Miss Lou) 66
best-sellers 38
Bhabha, Homi 17, 20–1, 22,
  24, 25
Bhaduri, Bhuvaneswari 19
Bhanot, Kavita 5
Black liberation movement, US
  105, 106, 112–13
Black Lives Matter 1–2, 49,
  51
Black Panther Party 112
Boochani, Behrouz 102, 115,
  116, 120–4
Booker Prize 117
bourgeoisie 14, 29–30
Bower, Rachel 134
Brathwaite, Kamau 56, 65–6,
  67–8, 141
Brennan, Timothy 26, 74, 108
British empire/imperialism 1–2
  and curriculum 35, 43–4,
  49–50
  and history 11–16, 48–50,
  67–8
  and reading 88–91, **92**
Brontë, Charlotte, *Jane Eyre*
  79, 84–6, **91–2**
Brownback, Sam 144

Index

calypso 66, **68**
Cambridge Companion to African-American Literature 37
Cambridge Companion to Postcolonial Literary Studies 37
Cambridge University 2–3, 35
Camus, Albert 81, 93, 94–6, 99, **101**
canon formation 34–41
  see also texts, canonical
Cape Town University 1–2
capitalism 6
  anti-capitalism 27, 87, 103, 115, 137
  and political argument 19–20, 110, 112, 158n21
capitalism, racial 112, 158n21
Caribbean 56, 63–9, 137, 139–41
Caribbean English/creole 56, 64, 65, 139
Casanova, Pascale 23
caste 60
Césaire, Aimé 23–4, 26, **32**
  Une tempête 79, 82, 89–91, **92**
Chaudhuri, Amit 56, 61
Chauka, Please Tell Us the Time (film) 121
Cobham, Rhonda 141
Coetzee, J. M., *Foe* 79, 82–4, 86, **91–2**
'Colonial countryside' project 50
colonialism
  and activism 1–2, 78, 152–3
  and antagonism 20, 22, 81
  and Caribbean 65–6, 137
  definition 156n2
  and education 14–15, 49, 60, 65, 88–9

and emancipation 82, 86, 132
and English literature 11–16, 21, 24
and freedom 89, 91, 99, 114
and genre 128, 133–4, **135**, 136–50, 138, 142, 144
and injustice 109, 111, 152–3
and language 73
  and Caribbean 56, 63–9, 139
  and English language 59, 63, 64, **68**, 68
  and literary technique 137, 138
  and literary tradition 133–4, **135**
neocolonialism 30, 59
and political argument 124–5, 138
and reading
  British 84–6, 88–91, **92**
  and emancipation 82, 86, **92**
  French 93–6, 97, 100, **101**
  and women 83, **101**
and reparation 138, 142, 144
and resistance 78, 102–26, 152–3
  anti-imperialism 30, 78, **92**
  and genre 128, 133, 136–50
  and postcolonial literary studies 19, 30, **32**
and translation 70, **76**
and women 19, 83, **101**
  and resistance 98, **101**
  and silencing **25**, 98, 99–100, **101**

Index

violence against women
97–100, **101**, 107–8,
110–11
see also anticolonialism
colonialism, European 2,
17–20, 21, 133, 152
French 93–6, 97, 100, **101**
colonialism, settler 94–6, 97,
101, 144, 152
Communist Party, US 105, 112
community 75, 77, 88
language communities 30,
59–60, **63, 66, 68**
Conrad, Joseph 21, 79, 86,
87–8, **92**
'contrapuntal', definition 80
see also reading,
contrapuntal
countryside, English 49–50
creole 64, 65
'crime scene forensics' 138
culture, colonial 28, 65, 87,
152
culture, national 28–30, **32**
culture, pre-colonial 59–60,
63, 135, 139–41
culture wars 35, 48
curriculum 1, 2, 4, 8, 16–17,
33–53
and African literature 39,
157n5
and diversification 35–6, 39,
81, 156n3
and exclusion 42, 50–1
and political argument 46,
47
and racism 35, 42, 45, 48,
49–52
and readership 30, 31, 39,
52
and reading 52, 54
and tools for decolonization
42
discussion 43, 46, 47

modules options 43–4, 47
teaching methods 43, 47
United Kingdom 12–14, 35
and British empire/
imperialism 43–4, 50
United States 4, 36
and world literature 36,
38
and writers of colour 35,
36, 37, 38, 48, 49–50

Dabashi, Hamid 73–4
Daily Telegraph 35
Dakota Access Pipeline 145
Dakota people 142, 144,
159n28
Damrosch, David 23
Davis, Angela 102, 105, 106,
111–12
De'Ath, Amy 47–8
Deckard, Sharae 129
decoloniality, definition 6, 7
'Decolonising SOAS' toolkit
33, 42–4
Decolonising SOAS Working
Group 42
decolonization, aesthetic 131
decolonization, cultural 32,
40, 87
decolonization of literature
see colonialism; English
literature; genre;
language; political
argument; postcolonial
literary studies; reading;
resistance
deconstruction 19, **25**
Defoe, Daniel, *Robinson
Crusoe* 79, 83–4, **91–2**
Delacroix, Eugène 97, 99
Derrida, Jacques 19, 20, **25**
Devi, Mahasweta 19
Dickens, Charles 17
'Diction' (Long Soldier) 143

184 Index

didacticism 26, 28
difference 20, **25**
discussion, open 43, 46, 47
disillusionment 22, 153
diversification
    and curriculum 35–6, 39,
        81, 156n3
    and world literature 23, 24
Djebar, Assia 81, 94, 96–7,
    101
    *Femmes d'Alger dans leur
        appartement* 93, 97–9
domination, colonial 21–2
    and English language 63,
        64, 68
domination, imperial 19, 92
domination, male 19–20
domination, neocolonial 59
domination, political and social
    29–30
drama 133
    Fireworks (Taha) 136, 137,
        149–50
    Keffiyeh/Made in China
        (Taha) 136, 137, 138,
        146–9
    Tempest (Shakespeare) 79,
        86, 88–91, **92**
    Une tempête (Césaire) 79,
        82, 89–91, **92**

Eagleton, Terry 13, 17
education
    and colonialism 14–15, 49,
        60, 65, 88–9
    and language of choice 58,
        60, 97
    and political argument
        109–10, 113, 114
    and reading 88–9, 97
egalitarianism 125
emancipation 82, 86, **92**, 132
    see also freedom
emotion 108–9, 112

The Empire Strikes Back (film)
    79
English language 3, 9, 12–13,
    29, 38, 132
    Achebe 56, 58–9, 67
    and Caribbean 56, 63–9, 139
    creole 64, 65
    and colonialism 63, 64, 68,
        68
    and Indigenous Americans
        138, 143
    and language 55–6, 58–62,
        67–8
        and Indian languages 56,
            61, 117
    and political argument 105,
        122
    and translation 45, **63**, 69,
        74, 122
English literature 5, 34–41
    and autonomy 13–14, **16**
    and colonialism 11–16, 21,
        24
    English Literature GCSE 13,
        14
    and institutionalization 12,
        130
    see also curriculum
Englishness 12, 50
environment, natural 84, 115,
    124, 125, 140, 155
environmental movement,
    transnational 102
Equiano, Olaudah 38
essays *see* Achebe, Chinua;
        Brathwaite, Kamau;
        Djebar, Assia; Fanon,
        Frantz; Ngũgĩ wa
        Thiong'o; Anyumba,
        Henry Owuor; Liyong,
        Taban Lo; Roy,
        Arundhati; Rushdie,
        Salman; Spivak, Gayatri
        Chakravorty

Index

Etherington, Ben 23, 134
ethnic minority writing 3, 4,
  35, 36, 38
ethnicity 60–1, 71
Eurocentrism 2, 4, 6–7, 18, 70,
  131
European colonialism 2,
  17–20, 21, 133, 152
  French 93–6, 97, 100, 101
European languages 29, 32, 72
  French 64, 97, 100
  Spanish 64
European literature 4, 17, 24,
  27, 78
exclusion, social 42, 50–1
experimentation, literary 26,
  127, 136–50
  and genre 127, 129, 130,
    136–50
  and identity 48, 146–7
  and layout 143, 145
  and literary technique 137,
    143, 145, 147–8
  and political argument 47–8,
    137, 142–3, 146–7, 148,
    149–50
  and resistance 145–7, 148

Fanon, Frantz
  and postcolonial literary
    studies 21, 30, 31
  'On National Culture'
    28–9, 32
  and reading 85, 94
Featherstone, David 108
Femmes d'Alger dans leur
  appartement (Djebar)
  93, 97–9
'fetishism of language' 56
fiction 124
  Indian 56, 61, 63
  see also novels
Fiorenza, Elisabeth Schüssler
  123

Fireworks (Taha) 136, 137,
  149–50
Flanagan, Richard 122
Foe (Coetzee) 79, 82–4, 86,
  91–2
Foucault, Michel 18, 20
Fowler, Corinne 49
freedom 89, 91, 99, 114
  see also emancipation
French imperialism/colonialism
  93–6, 97, 100, 101
French language 64, 97, 100
Frente Sandinista de Liberación
  Nacional (FSLN) 104–5,
  158n17
Freud, Sigmund 20
Front de Libération Nationale
  (FLN) 28, 93, 94, 95,
  98, 99
future vision
  Fanon 29, 32
  and political argument 103,
    111–12, 115, 129
  and writing back 82, 87, 91

Gardiner, Michael 12
General Certificate of
  Secondary Education
  (GCSE), UK 13, 14
genre 8, 127–50
  autobiography 104–14, 122
  and capitalism 110, 112,
    158n21
  and liberation movements
    108, 112–13
  and colonialism 128, 133–4,
    135, 136–50
  and history 129, 133–4,
    142, 143
  and imperial violence 138,
    144, 149–50
  and information provision
    127, 128
  and language 132, 136–50

Index

genre (*cont.*)
  and literary experimentation
      127, 129, 130, 136–50
  and modernism 127, 130,
      135, 136–7
  novels 128, 133–4, 141
  poetry 133, 134, 142–5
  and postmodernism 130,
      135
  and readership 128, 130–1,
      135, 138–9
  and reparation 138, 142,
      144
  and resistance 128, 130–50
    anticolonialism 128, 133,
      136–50
    and literary
      experimentation 145–7,
      148
    short stories 128, 133,
      139–41
    'La femme adultère'
      (Camus) 93, 94, **101**
  and Western literature
      130–2, **135**
  and women writers 136
  see also essays; technique,
      literary; tradition,
      literary
Gikandi, Simon 157n11
Gĩkũyũ language 29, 59–60
Gilmour, Rachael 72
God of Small Things (Roy) 29
Goebel, Walter 130, 131
Goethe, Johann Wolfgang von,
      Weltliteratur 23
Gopal, Priyamvada 7, 61, 62,
      93, 100
Gorky, Maxim 110
Griffiths, Gareth 79
Guevara, Che 104, 108

Hajjar, George 105
harems 97–9

Harlow, Barbara 30, **32**, 103,
      106
Harris, Wilson 87, **92**
Haymarket Books 106
'He Sápa' (Long Soldier) 142–3
Heart of Darkness (Conrad)
      79, 86, 87–8, **92**
Helgesson, Stefan 7
heritage, African-Caribbean
      65–6, **68**, 139–41
  and language 56, 64, 65–6
heritage, English 48–50
  literary heritage 13–15, **16**
heritage, literary 13–15, **16**,
      97
heritage studies 48–9
history 6
  and genre 129, 133–4, 142,
      143
  and imperialism
    and British empire/
      imperialism 11–16,
      48–50, 67–8
    and reading 81, 82
    and language of choice 58,
      67–8, **69**
    and reading 81, 82, 83, 92,
      97
history, alternative **92**
history, institutional 8, 11–32
history, Palestinian 146–7,
      149–50
Hitchcock, Peter 133
hooks, bell 50
human rights 116
  see also refugees; women's
      rights
humanitarianism 116, 148,
      149
hybridity 20, 21, **25**

identity 20–1
  and literary experimentation
      48, 146–7

Index

and reading 84–6, 96
and writers of colour 38, 127
identity, group 5, 48
identity, national 50, 87, 96, 146–7
identity, racial 48
identity politics 48
Igbo society 88
ijtihad 75
imagery 103, 134, 139
imagination, freedom of 14–15
imperialism 1–2, 11–20
anti-imperialism 7, 27, 137, 156n2
anti-imperial struggle/ resistance 30, 78, 92
and curriculum 43–4, 50
definition 156n2
and history 11–16, 48–50, 67–8, 81, 82
and imperial domination 19, 92
and imperial violence 22, 100, 115, 138
Algeria 93, 99
and silencing **91**, 98, 99, **101**
and writing back 82, 83, 84, 85–6, **91**
and reading 80
British 88–91, **92**
and contrapuntal reading 93–6, 98, 99, 100, **101**
French 93–6, 97, 100, **101**
and history 81, 82
and imperial violence 83, 84, 85–6, **91**, 98, 99, 100, 101
and writing back 79, 82, 83, 84, 86–7, 88–91, **92**
and silencing 19–20, **25**, **91**
and women **25**, 98, 99–100, **101**

and subaltern people 19–20, **25**
see also British empire/ imperialism
imperialism, capitalist 6, 8, 19–20, **25**
imperialism, European 17–18, 19–20
French 93–6, 97, 100, **101**
impoverishment of universities 157n5
independence, political 6–7, 29, 65, 78, 99
Algeria 28, 93, 94, **101**
India 12
Indian languages 60–1, 62, 63, 72
Indigenous people
Indigenous Americans 64, 138, 142–4, 152
and pre-colonial tradition 92, 134, 138, 142–6
and reparation 138, 142, 144
inequalities
and language 57, **63**, 76
and political argument 109–10, 119–20
information 43, 127, 128
injustice 109, 111, 152–3
innovation 132, 134–5
institutionalization, academic 12, 130
interpretation 48, 55, 75
Iran 120–1
Ireland 12
Ishiguro, Kazuo 13, 38
Israel 73, 158n12
Israeli–Palestinian conflict 45–6, 152–3

Jalada writers' collective 74
Jarvis, Jill 93
Jawad, Rania 146
Jelloun, Tahar Ben 97

Index

Johnson, Linton Kwesi 66
journalism 117–18, 121,
  152–3
Jovenes Socialistas 110

Kanafani, Ghassan 31, **32**,
  45–6
Keffiyeh/Made in China (Taha)
  136, 137, 138, 146–9
Kenya 14–15, 40, 59
Khaled, Leila 102, 104, 105,
  107–8
Kilito, Abdelfatah 31
Kincaid, Jamaica 127, 136–41
Knepper, Wendy 129
knowledge, personal 43, 46,
  131–2
Krishnan, Madhu 9
Kurdish people 120–1, 124
Kureishi, Hanif 36
'kyriarchy' 123

'La femme adultère' (Camus)
  93, 94, **101**
Laachir, Karima 72
Lacan, Jacques 20
Lakota people 138, 142–3
  Dakota 142, 144, 159n28
  Oglala Lakota 127, 136,
    142–4, 159n28
language 8, 58–69, 76, 122,
  136–50
  African languages **32**, 62,
    63, 65–6, 72, 89
  Gĩkũyũ 29, 59–60
  and Ngũgĩ wa Thiong'o
    30, **32**, 56, 59–60, **63**,
    157n11
  Swahili 39, 89
  African literature 29–30, **32**,
    58–60, 62, 72
  and African-Caribbean
    cultural heritage 63–9,
    139

'nation language' 66, **68**,
  69
Philip 56, 63–4, 66, 67–8,
  69
Arabic 94–5, 100, 136
and colonialism 73
and Caribbean 56, 63–9,
  139
and English language 59,
  63, 64, 68
and European colonialism
  60, 94–5, 133, 143–6,
  147–8
and education 58, 60, 97
European languages 29, **32**,
  72
French 64, 97, 100
Spanish 64
Farsi 122
and genre 132, 136–50
and history 58, 67–8, **69**
Indigenous languages 138,
  143–6
and inequalities 57, **63**, **76**
and literary technique 65,
  66, **68**, 137, 138, 142,
  143
and multilingualism 54, 58,
  72–3
and oral tradition 66, **68**
and particularity 30, 62, 71
and readership 58, 61, **63**,
  75
and reading 54, 89, 94–5,
  100
and self-expression 47, 59
and social class 58, 60–1
South Asian 60–1, **62**, **63**,
  72, 128
and world literature 69, 70,
  76, 157n9
see also English language;
  pre-colonial languages;
  translation, literary

Index

language abilities 70, 71, 132, 143–4
language communities 30, 59–60, **63, 66, 68**
language of law 144
Latin American studies 6
layout 143, 145
Lazarus, Neil 4, 22
Leavis, F. R. 14
Leavis, Q. D. 14
'Legacies of British Slavery' database 50
liberalism 7
liberation movements 6, 22
  Black liberation movement 105, 106, 112–13
  Palestinian 31, 45, 104, 108
  and political argument 105, 108, 112–13
  Sandinistas 104, 110, 111
Liberation School, Los Angeles 113
liberation struggle, national 23, **25**, 45
  Algeria 94, 95, 99, **101**
  see also Front de Libération Nationale (FLN)
liberationism, national 22, 23, **25**
liminality 21
Lincoln, Abraham 143
literary criticism 79, 131, 132, 154–5
literary studies 3, 8, 11–32, 33–53, 106–7
  and Fanon 21, 28–9, 30, 31, **32**
  and political argument 26, 27–9
  see also postcolonial literary studies
literary theory, classical 130
literary traditions see tradition, literary

literature, anglophone see anglophone literature
literature, comparative 78–101, 131
  and translation 70, 71, 73
  see also reading; writing back
literature, definition of 26
literature, English see English literature
literature, experimental see experimentation, literary
literature, Western 130–2, **135**
Liyong, Taban Lo 33, 39, 40–3
location 40, 139
Loh, Lucienne 49–50
LoLordo, V. Nicholas 37, 38
London 43, 44
Long Soldier, Layli 127, 136–7, 138, 142–5
Los Angeles Times 137, 138

McLeod, John 130
Mahfouz, Naguib 69, 96
Mammywata ('River Mumma') (water spirit) 138, 140–1
manifestos for decolonization 41–2
Mannoni, Octave 88–9
Manus Island, Australia 116, 121, 123, 124–5
Manus Recording Project Collective 121
maqama 159n25
marginalized people/groups 35–6, 88
  subaltern people 19–20, **25**
Mariátegui, José Carlos 31
Marxism 21, 110, 157n11
Marzagora, Sara 72
Mbembe, Achille 1–2
mega-dams 116, 118
melodrama 119–20
Mer-Khamis, Julian 138
Mignolo, Walter 6, 7

Index

migrant refugees 151–2
and political argument 21,
102, 116
and social movements
121, 122, 123, 124–5
mimesis 130
mimicry 20, **25**
missionary work 88
modernism
and genre 127, 130, **135**,
136–7
and postcolonial literary
studies 26, 29, **32**
modernity, capitalist 6
module options 35–6, **41**,
43–4, 47
Moore-Gilbert, Bart 21
Moretti, Franco 23
Mufti, Aamir 23
Mullen, Harryette 48
multilingualism 54, 58, 72–3

Nairobi University 40, 157n5
Narayan, R. K. 62
'nation language' 66, **68**, 69
National Trust 48–9
nativism, cultural 40
Négritude movement 28
neocolonialism 30, 59
neoliberalism 116, 119–20
neutrality 60–1, 81
New Yorker magazine 138
Ngũgĩ wa Thiong'o
and Anyumba, Henry Owuor
and Liyong, Taban Lo
33, 39, 40–3
Decolonising the Mind 7,
29–30
and postcolonial literary
studies 14–15, 17,
29–30, 31
and pre-colonial languages
30, **32**, 56, 59–60, **63**,
74–5, 157n11

and reading 79, 93
Nicaragua 31, 104, 109,
158n17
Nigeria 88
Niranjana, Tejaswini 70
Nixon, Rob 116
No Friend but the Mountains
(Boochani) 116, 120–4
Nobel Prize for Literature 38,
96–7
*Norton Anthology of English
Literature* 36–7, 38,
157n4
*Norton Anthology of Modern
and Contemporary
Poetry* 38
Norton Anthology of Poetry
36, 37, 157n4
novelization 119
novels 127, 128, 133–4, 141

Obama, Barack 144
Occupy Wall Street 120
Olufemi, Lola 35
'On National Culture' (Fanon)
28–9, **32**
oppression 116, 123, 124–5
Orientalism 97–8
and postcolonial literary
studies 17–18, 21–2, 23,
24–5
Orsini, Francesca 72
otherness, colonial 21
out of print texts 43
Oxford University 1

Palestine 31, 44–6, 146–53
'Palestinian and Israeli
Literature' module 44–5
Palestinian national liberation
movement 31, 45, 108
parody 130
Parry, Benita 22, 80
particularity 30, 62, 71

Index

patois/patwa 64
patriarchy 98, 100
Pedagogies for Social Justice
   project, UK 157n6
Penguin Books 106
periodization, historical 4
Perkins, Margo 106
persuasion, techniques of 112,
   118
Philip, M. NourbeSe 56, 63–4,
   66, 67–8, **69**
Picasso, Pablo 99
poetry 47, 139, 142–5
   and literary tradition 133,
      134
   and political argument 124,
      142–3
poiesis 130
politics, identity 48
political argument 8, 102–26,
   155
   and autobiography 104–14,
      122
   and capitalism 110, 112,
      158n21
   and liberation movements
      108, 112–13
   and violence against
      women 107–8, 110–11
   and awareness 113, 114,
      118
   and capitalism 19–20, 110,
      112, 158n21
   and colonialism 124–5, 138
   and curriculum 46, 47
   and education 109–10, 113,
      114
   and emotion 108–9, 112
   and English language 105,
      122
   and future vision 103, 115,
      129
   and imperial violence 106,
      115, 123, 124

and inequality 109–10,
   119–20
and injustice 109, 111
and literary experimentation
   47–8, 137, 142–3,
   146–7, 148, 149–50
and literary technique 103,
   108–9, 111, 117–19,
   124, **135**, 138
and literary traditions 122,
   124, 131–2, **135**
and migrant refugees 21,
   102, 116
and social movements
   121, 122, 123, 124–5
and neoliberalism 116,
   119–20
and oppression 116, 123,
   124–5
and persuasion 112, 118
and poetry 124, 142–3
and postcolonial literary
   studies 26, 27–31, **32**
and readership 103, 109,
   112, 116, 118–19
and resistance 104–14, 115–26
   and literary experimentation
      146–7, 148
   and social movements 116,
      118, 121, 122, 123,
      124–5
   liberation movements 105,
      108, 112–13
and stereotyping 46, 123
and style of writing 108–9,
   111, 117–19, 124
and tools for decolonization
   46, 47–8
and translation 115–16, 122
politics of translation 70, **76**
Popular Front for the
   Liberation of Palestine
   (PFLP) 45, 104, 105,
   158n19

Index

postcolonial literary studies 3–4, 17, 25–32, 34–41
  and ambivalence 20, 22, 25
  and bourgeoisie 14, 29–30
  and Fanon 21, 28–9, 30, 31, 32
  and modernism 26, 29, 32
  and module options 35–6, 41, 43–4, 47
  and national liberationism 22, 23, 25
  and Ngũgĩ wa Thiong'o 14–15, 17, 29–30, 31
  and Orientalism 17–18, 21–2, 23, 24–5
  and political argument 26, 27–31, 32
  and postmodernism 26, 32
  and representation 19–20, 22
  and resistance 21, 22
  and Said 20, 21–2, 23, 24–5, 26
  and silencing 19–20, 25
  and social class 14, 29–30, 32
  and Spivak 17, 19–20, 21, 22, 24, 25
  see also literary studies; world literature
postcolonial literature 4, 19
  see also world literature
postmodernism 26, 32, 130, 135
Pravinchandra, Shital 128
pre-colonial languages 147–8
  African languages 32, 39, 62, 63, 65–6, 72, 89
  Gĩkũyũ 29, 59–60
  Arabic 94–5, 100
  Farsi 122
  Indian languages 60–1, 62, 63, 72
  Indigenous people 138, 145

and Ngũgĩ wa Thiong'o 30, 32, 56, 59–60, 63, 74–5, 157n11
pre-colonial traditions see tradition, literary
Présence Africaine (publishers) 27
Project Myopia 157n6
'prose poems' 139
protest see activism; liberation movements; resistance; social movements
psychoanalytic theory 20, 25
publishing industry 5, 43, 48, 56

Quijano, Aníbal 6
Quinault people 152

racism 1–2, 5, 27
  and curriculum 35, 42, 45, 48, 49–52
  racial capitalism 112, 158n21
  structural 42, 48, 152
  and writing back 86, 88
Ramazani, Jahan 38
Randall, Margaret 105
Random House (publishers) 106
Rao, Nagesh 119
readership
  and anglophone literature 30, 31, 61, 130–1, 135
  and curriculum 30, 31, 39, 52
  and genre 128, 130–1, 135, 138–9
  and language 58, 61, 63, 75
  and political argument 103, 109, 112, 116, 118–19
reading 8, 78–101, 153–4
  Achebe 79, 82, 87–8, 92
  and canonical texts 79, 83, 86, 91–2

and colonialism
  and British imperialism
    84–6, 88–91, **92**
  and emancipation 82, 86,
    92
  and French imperialism
    93–6, 97, 100, **101**
  and women 83, **101**
  and curriculum 52, 54
  and education 88–9, 97
  and history 81, 82, 83, 92,
    97
  and identity 84–6, 96
  and imperial violence 82, 83,
    84, 85–6, **91**
  Algeria 93, 97–100, **101**
  and silencing **91**, 97–100,
    101
  violence against women
    97–100, **101**, 107–8,
    110–11
and imperialism 80
  British 88–91, **92**
  and contrapuntal reading
    93–6, 100, **101**
  French 93–6, 97, 99–100,
    101
  and history 81, 82
  and silencing **91**, 98,
    99–100, **101**
  and writing back 79, 82,
    83, 84, 86–7, 88–91, **92**
and interpretation 48, 55, 75
and language 54
  pre-colonial languages 89,
    94–5, 100
and patriarchy 98, 100
and Said 79, 80, 81, 92, 94,
    96
and Spivak 83, 84
and writing back 82–92
and relationships 100, **101**
reading, contrapuntal 8, 78,
    80, 92–101

reading, situated 75–6, **77**
reading lists 5, 37, 43, 51
reading widely 15, **16**, 92–3,
    130–1
realism, literary 130
refugees *see* migrant refugees
relationships between texts
    100, **101**
reparation 138, 142, 144
reportage, anticolonial
    internationalist 117–18
representation 19–20, 22
resistance 102–26
  and colonialism 78, 102–26,
    152–3
  anti-imperialism 30, 78,
    92
  and genre 128, 133,
    136–50
  and postcolonial literary
    studies 19, 30, **32**
and genre 128, 130–50
  anticolonialism 128, 133,
    136–50
  and literary
    experimentation 145–7,
    148
  and political argument
    104–14, 115–26
  and literary
    experimentation 146–7,
    148
  and postcolonial literary
    studies 21, 22
  and women 98, **101**
  see also activism; liberation
    movements; social
    movements
resistance, Black 50
resistance, collective 75, 113,
    119
'resistance literature' 30–1, **32**,
    46, 66, 103
'rhetorical excess' 119

Rhodes, Cecil 1–2
Rhys, Jean, *Wide Sargasso Sea* 79, 82–3, 84–6, **91–2**
rhythm 65, 66, **68**
Robinson Crusoe (Defoe) 79, 83–4, **91–2**
Romains, Jules 27
Romantics, British 13–14
Roy, Arundhati 61, 102, 115, 116, 117–20
Royal Court Theatre 146–7
Rushdie, Salman 21, 26, 36, 79
and language 56, 61, 62
Russia 151–2

Said, Edward 75
Orientalism 17–18, **24**
and postcolonial literary studies 20, 21–2, 23, **24–5**, 26
and reading 79, 80, 81, 92
and Camus 94, 96
Salem, François Abu 138
Salih, Tayeb 87, **92**
sanctions, economic 152
Sandinistas 104, 110, 111
sarcasm 118
Sardar Sarovar mega-dam, Gujarat 116, 118
sati, act of 19
Schabio, Saskia 130, 131
Scotland 12
security companies, private 116, 121
self-expression 47, 59
settlers, European 144, 152
French 94–6, 97, **101**
Shakespeare, William 13
Tempest 79, 86, 88–91, **92**
Shankar, S. 61–2
silencing
and imperial violence **91**, 97–100, **101**

and postcolonial studies 19–20, **25**
and women **25**, 98, 99–100, **101**
S.J.Res. 14 144, 142
slavery 17, 36, 48–9, 50, 51
and Caribbean 64, 65, 67, 84–6, 137
Smith, Linda Tuhiwai 1, 5
Smith, Zadie 37, 38
SOAS University of London 33, 42
social class 5, 109–10
and language 58, 60–1
and postcolonial literary studies 14, 29–30, **32**
social control 12, 15, **16**
social movements 1–3, 43–4, 115–26
Black liberation movement 105, 106, 112–13
Black Lives Matter 1–2, 49, 51
and translation 75, **76**, 116
socialism 7, 22, 30
Soledad Brothers 113
Somoza regime 104, 110–11
South Africa 1–2, 31
South Asian languages 60–1, **62**, **63**, 72, 128
sovereignty, political 13, 24
Spanish language 64
Spivak, Gayatri Chakravorty 56, 131
and postcolonial literary studies 17, 19–20, 21, 22, **24**, **25**
and reading 70–1, 83, 84
Stanford University 35
statues 1–2
stereotyping 46, 123, 138
stories, short 128, 133, 139–41
'La femme adultère' (Camus) 93, 94, **101**

Index

195

struggle *see* resistance
Student Nonviolent
 Coordinating Committee
 (SNCC) 112
style 139
 and literary experimentation
  143, 147–8
 and political argument
  108–9, 111, 117–19,
  124
subaltern people 19–20, **25**
subversion 130
surrealism, horrific 124
Swahili 39, 89
Syal, Meera 13
syntax 65, 66, 83, 143

Taha, Dalia 127, 136–7
 Fireworks 136, 137, 149–50
 Keffiyeh/Made in China 136,
  137, 138, 146–9
teaching methods 43, 47
technique, literary 134–5
 and colonialism 137, 138
 imagery 103, 134, 139
 and language 65, 66, **68**, 83,
  137, 138, 142, 143
 layout 143, 145
 and literary experimentation
  137, 143, 145, 147–8
 and political argument
  108–9, 111, 117–19,
  124, **135**, 138
 rhythm 65, 66, **68**
 style 108–9, 111, 117–19,
  124, 139, 143, 147–8
 syntax 65, 66, 83, 143
 vocabulary 83, 103, 108
Tempest (Shakespeare) 79, 86,
 88–91, **92**
texts, canonical 34–41
 canonization 13, 83
 traditional English 3–4, 5,
  14, 15, **16**

 and reading 79, 83, 86,
  91–2
 Western 131, 132, **135**
texts, experimental *see*
 experimentation,
 literary
Things Fall Apart (Achebe) 79,
 82, 87–8
Tiffin, Helen 79
Tijerino Haslam, Doris 104–6,
 109–11
Tofighian, Omid 121–3, 124
toolkits for decolonization 42,
 43
torture 107–8, 110–11, 116,
 123
tourism 137
tradition, civic 26
tradition, literary 130–6, 154
 and colonialism 133–4, **135**
 English canonical texts 3–4,
  5, 14, 15, **16**
 and reading 79, 83, 86,
  91–2
 and innovation 132, 134–5
 and literature, Western
  130–2, **135**
 and political argument 122,
  124, 131–2, **135**
 see also heritage,
  African-Caribbean
tradition, oral 124, 133, 134,
 141
 and language 66, **68**
tradition, pre-colonial **92**,
 134, 138, 141, 142–6,
 159n25
translation, literary 8, 38, 55,
 69–77
 and colonialism 70, **76**
 and communication 71–2,
  73–4, 75–6, **77**
 and comparative literature
  70, 71, 73

translation, literary (*cont.*)
and English language 45, **63**,
69, 74, 122
and political argument
115–16, 122
and pre-colonial literature
61, **63**
pros and cons of 56–7, 73–4
and social movements 75,
76, 116
untranslatability 71
translation, politics of 70, **76**
'trickledown economics' 119
Tuck, Eve 156n1
Twyman, Richard 147

Ukraine 151–2
Une tempête (Césaire) 79, 82,
89–91, **92**
United Kingdom *see* British
empire/imperialism;
curriculum; English
language; English
literature
United States 4, 35, 36, 72, 143
United States Congress 142,
144
universalism 23–4, 30
universities, African 157n5
universities, metropolitan
anglophone 4, 16–17,
37, 52
and African literature 39,
157n5
and diversification 35–6,
156n3
and exclusion, social 42,
50–1
and white supremacism
35–6, 156n3
untranslatability 71

values, human 14–15
Varma, Rashmi 118

vernacular languages 62
see also pre-colonial
languages
violence, imperial 22
and genre 138, 144, 149–50
and political argument 106,
107–8, 110–11, 115,
123, 124
and reading 82, 83, 84,
85–6, **91**
Algeria 93, 97–100, **101**
and silencing **91**, 97–100,
101
violence against women
97–100, **101**, 107–8,
110–11
torture 107–8, 110–11, 116,
123
Viswanathan, Gauri 12, 15,
17, 34

Walcott, Derek 37
Wales 12
Ward, Jonathan 50, 51–2
Warwick Research Collective
56, 73
Welch, James 143
Weltliteratur (Goethe) 23
Wenzel, Jennifer 22
Werya magazine 121
Westall, Claire 5
Wheatley, Phyllis 37
'Whereas' (Long Soldier) 142,
144–5
white readers 39
white settlers 94–6, 97
white supremacism 2, 35, 152,
156n3
whiteness 12
Wide Sargasso Sea (Rhys) 79,
82–3, 84–6, **91–2**
'wokery' 49
women 19, 83, **101**
and resistance 98, **101**

Index

and silencing 25, 98, 99–100, **101**
violence against women 97–100, **101**, 107–8, 110–11
women, Algerian 81, 94, 97–100, **101**
women writers 35, 100, 136–50
women's autobiographies 104–14
women's rights 99–100, **101**
working class 30, **32**
World Bank 118
world literature 4, 17, 23, 25, 80, 128
 and curriculum 35, 38
 and diversification 23, **24**
 and language 69, 70, **76**, 157n9
 see also postcolonial literary studies
writers, Black *see* writers of colour
writers, Caribbean 63–9
writers, metropolitan 43

writers, multilinguistic 58, 72–3
writers, South Asian 60
writers, well-known 38
writers, white 35, 38, 47–8
writers, women 35, 100, 136–50
writers of colour 35, 48, 49–50, 63–9
 in anthologies 36, 37, 38
 and identity 38, 127
writing back 78–9, 82–92
 and future vision 82, 87, 91
 and imperialism 79, 82, 83, 84, 86–7, 88–91, **92**
 and racism 86, 88
 and relationships between texts 100, **101**
'Writing London' module 44
'Writing Race, Writing Gender' module 47

Yang, K. Wayne 156n1

Zimbler, Jarad 84, 134